The
PENNSYLVANIA
WILDS
AND THE
CIVIL WAR

KATHY MYERS

THE
History
PRESS

Published by The History Press
Charleston, SC
www.historypress.com

First published 2023

Manufactured in the United States

ISBN 9781467153072

Library of Congress Control Number: 2022950077

Notice: The information in this book is true and complete to the best of our knowledge. It is offered without guarantee on the part of the author or The History Press. The author and The History Press disclaim all liability in connection with the use of this book.

To Andrew, Henry and John:

"I saw before me those who are to come. I looked back and saw my father, and his father, and all our fathers, and in front to see my son, his son, and the sons upon sons beyond. And their eyes were my eyes. As I felt, so they had felt and were to feel, as then, so now, as tomorrow and forever. Then I was not afraid, for I was in a long line that had no beginning and no end, and the hand of his father grasped my father's hand, and his hand was in mine, and my unborn son took my right hand, and all, up and down the line that stretched from Time That Was to Time That Is, and Is Not Yet, raised their hands to show the link, and we found that we were one, born of Woman, Son of Man, made in the Image, fashioned in the Womb by the Will of God, the Eternal Father. I was one of them, they were of me, and in me, and I in all of them."

—How Green Was My Valley,
by Richard Llewellyn (Macmillan Company, 1940)

CONTENTS

Contents

PREFACE

The Pennsylvania Wilds is home to only 4 percent of the population of Pennsylvania. I am the seventh generation of my family to live in the region. That's a lot of history!

Our ancestors were extraordinary people, exemplifying the Commonwealth's motto, "Virtue, Liberty and Independence."[1] In an earlier book, *Historic Tales of the Pennsylvania Wilds*, I wrote about Pennsylvania from its founding, through the French and Indian War of 1755, the American Revolution and the exploration of the Last Purchase of 1784 that encompasses the Pennsylvania Wilds and led to its settlement.

As the region grew, I questioned what other challenges its residents faced and how they reacted. Moving into the time of the Civil War, research provided new information on the people who populated the Wilds in those years. From abolitionists to Copperheads, from patriotic volunteer soldiers to deserters, the Wilds had them all. It also had an extensive Underground Railroad system, with many people acting as conductors and stationmasters, people willing to defy the federal Fugitive Slave Acts of 1793 and 1850 to help those desperate to be free to pass through the region on their way to Canada. The Wilds had average citizens who volunteered for military service, women who were not nurses but acted as nurses and those who remained on the homefront. There were many heroic figures as well as some surprises, such as abolitionist Thomas L. Kane, who formed the famous regiments known as the Bucktails; Sarah Elizabeth Simcox of Clinton County, who served as a nurse and as a teenager in Bellefonte was an acquaintance of

Ulysses Grant before he became a famous general; John Wilkes Booth and his oilman connection; Ely Parker, a Seneca Indian who helped write the terms of Lee's surrender; and, whether fact or fiction, the lost Civil War gold shipment of Elk County.

Small in population, the people of the Wilds stepped up to help preserve the Union.

INTRODUCTION

On a sunny November day, sitting at my writing desk in my home on Hemlock Hill in the Pennsylvania Wilds, the country had just turned out to vote, and I was waiting to learn the results of the election of our forty-sixth president of the United States, incumbent president Donald Trump or former vice president Joe Biden. Commentators and journalists said that this was the most critical election in the history of the country, noting that at no time had the country been so deeply divided.

As a historian and one who has been interested in politics since the young age of nine, I questioned whether this really was the most polarizing time the country has gone through. I believe that politics is part of our national DNA, something that the spirit of those who have gone before us have passed down as our legacy.

Both my husband and I had great-grandfathers and uncles, residents of the region known as the "Wilds," who served in the American Civil War. One would think that time was more polarizing than what we experienced during the 2020 election season. Interested in the stories of our ancestors and the stories of others who lived through the Civil War in the Pennsylvania Wilds, I turned my research to those years of conflict, especially how it affected people personally in this region of Pennsylvania.

Join me as we explore the Civil War years in the Pennsylvania Wilds.

Part I

PRELUDE TO CIVIL WAR

THE WILDS COMING OF AGE

The Pennsylvania Wilds is a special place in America, with fifty state game lands, twenty-nine state parks, nine state and national forests and sixteen thousand miles of streams and rivers....The Pennsylvania Wilds [is] *home to seventy percent of our nation's finest headwaters* [and] *to many people and industries who are able to make their living from the woods....It is also one of the largest expanses of green between New York City and Chicago.*[2]

Rebecca Harding Davis (1831–1910), American author and Pennsylvania native, captured the essence of the Wilds when she wrote, "Nowhere else in this country, from sea to sea, does nature comfort us with such assurance of plenty, such rich and tranquil beauty as in those unsung, unpainted hills of Pennsylvania."[3]

The Pennsylvania Wilds, composed of twelve and a half counties that cover 25 percent of the state, is home to only 4 percent of the state's population. These counties are Cameron, Clinton, Clarion, Clearfield, Elk, Forest, Jefferson, Lycoming, McKean, Potter, Tioga, Warren and northern Centre.[4]

What is the definition of "coming of age"? In today's society, it generally refers to the time when children pass into adulthood, by age or by experience, but in 1729, it would have been defined as "the attainment of prominence, respectability, recognition or maturity."[5]

Irvine United Presbyterian Church, Warren County, built in 1837. *National Register of Historic Places, National Park Service, Wikimedia Commons.*

As the author of an earlier book, *Historic Tales of the Pennsylvania Wilds*, I focused my attention on the period of time from the French and Indian War through the American Revolution, which led to settlement of the region known as the Last Purchase of 1784. That region included the counties that are today identified as the Pennsylvania Wilds. Life was challenging for the early settlers. With no roads to travel, they followed Indian paths to their destinations. Supplies were miles away, and the loneliness of a very isolated life was difficult, especially for women. Old farmers remembered the "Summerless Year of 1816," a freak of nature that froze crops in the northeast during the summer months as "eighteen hundred and starve to death."[6] An early Jefferson County inhabitant recalled living for a week on dried apples and cornbread. Having white wheat cakes at Christmas was a great treat. Another reminisced about a time when the family was so short on food they boiled pumpkin seeds, while another family lived on green corn for two weeks.[7]

Slowly, over time, life in the Wilds began to change. The institutions that we today take for granted and that define respectability began to develop. Take, for example, changes in the population. While colonial Pennsylvania was made up of immigrants primarily from England, Germany and Ireland, including Scotch-Irish, the years following the American Revolution and the opening of the Last Purchase provided opportunities for other immigrants. The 1850 census, the first that distinctly shows birthplace of our citizens, reveals that while many living in the region were native-born Pennsylvanians, most likely descendants of those who fought in the Revolution or the War of 1812, the records also reveal an influx of people from other states, particularly New York and the New England states. Here and there, new immigrants from England, Germany, Ireland, France and Belgium were also counted.

McKean County, which was formed from part of Lycoming County in 1804, had a population of 142 in 1810; however, by the year just prior to the Civil War, 1860, the population had expanded to 7,651.[8]

In 1842, in what was to become Elk County, the German Union Bond Society purchased thirty-five thousand acres of land from the U.S. Land Company, and by the fall of that year, thirty-one families from Germany had settled in a new community, Marienstadt, or St. Marys as it is known today. By the spring of 1843, thirty-three more families from Germany had joined them.[9] Elk County was established as a separate county in 1843.

Roadbuilding was another sign of progress. In place of Indian paths, residents made advances in establishing easier means for transportation. In Jefferson County, "Previous to the War of 1812 there were no roads; the 'Chinklacamoose Path' from Clearfield through Punxsutawney, and 'Meade's Trail' from Clearfield through Brookville westward were the only highways."[10] It appears that residents in 1809 petitioned Indiana County (which had jurisdiction over Jefferson County at that time) regarding the building of roads.[11] Between 1830 and 1840, residents continued petitioning the court to build principal roads and county bridges.[12]

Centre County Courthouse. Original section was built in 1805, with several additions over the years, including 1854–55. *Wikimedia Commons.*

Brookville Democrat, established in 1832. *From* Caldwell's Atlas of Jefferson County, Pennsylvania *(1878).*

Another sign of the Wilds "coming of age" was the court system. Court was first held in Lycoming County at Jaysburg in 1795 but was soon moved to Williamsport, with its first session held in 1796.[13] The first court in McKean County was held at Smethport on September 25, 1826.[14] In Elk County, the first court was not held in Ridgway, which is today's county

"Farmers High School, which is now Old Main in Pennsylvania State University, 1855."
Wikimedia Commons.

seat, but rather in a schoolhouse in Caledonia, with the court recording the date as December 19, 1843.[15] The first court in Forest County was held at Marienville in 1857.[16]

What is more prominent in society than having a means to circulate the news, in those early days through the medium of newspapers? In 1832, the first newspaper in Jefferson County, the *Jeffersonian Democrat*, began publication, a sure sign of progress.[17] In Clarion County, the *Clarion Democrat* began publication in 1838.[18] By 1849, the first newspaper had been established in Elk County. Named the *St. Marys Republican*, it lasted only a few weeks. More successful was the *Elk County Advocate*, first published in Ridgway on March 9, 1850.[19]

Meeting the religious needs of the residents of the Wilds were first handled by circuit riding ministers, who held services in people's homes or in schools until log churches were built to serve the congregation. As time went on, frame churches were erected; in the more established counties in the Wilds, churches were built of brick or stone, such as the magnificent St. James Episcopal Church in Muncy, Lycoming County, built between 1857 and 1859.[20]

St. James Episcopal Church, Muncy, built between 1857 and 1859. *National Register of Historic Places, Wikimedia Commons.*

As early as 1803 or 1804, a pioneer school had been established in Jefferson County in a building of rough logs with no windowpanes. The school term was three months.[21] Eventually, common schools were organized and grades established. Suitable blackboards and furnishings were made available. One township provided all of its schools with a *Webster's Unabridged Dictionary*.[22]

Pre–Civil War colleges in the Wilds region included Penn State in Centre County, the Commonwealth's only land grant university, chartered in 1855;[23] Lycoming College in Williamsport, Lycoming County, founded as the Williamsport Academy in 1812;[24] and Mansfield University in Tioga County, founded as Mansfield Academy in 1857.[25]

THE MISSOURI COMPROMISE, THE DRED SCOTT DECISION AND THE FUGITIVE SLAVE ACT

A house divided against itself cannot stand.
—*Abraham Lincoln, 1858*

Understanding the events that ultimately contributed to the Civil War requires a look back at actions taken by Congress and the courts.

Leading up to the Civil War, the North was an industrial region, with small farms worked by individual families. In contrast, the southern states were agricultural, with large plantations that relied heavily on enslaved labor. Both the North and South were seeking to extend their economic and political influence over new territories in the West.[26]

In 1820, when the settlement of the Wilds region was in its early stages, James Monroe was the fifth president of the United States, and his administration was often referred to as "the era of good feelings," which was characterized by a lack of political animosity and a period of national prosperity.[27] The "good feelings" followed in the aftermath of the War of 1812. First described by the *Boston Columbian Centinel* in July 12, 1817, it noted that the era began in 1815, when American citizens started to pay less attention to European political and military matters, what many today would refer to as isolationism.[28] The "era of good feelings" reflected a desire for unity in the country. But events in 1820 caused the North and South to clash openly and often on two central issues: extending slavery into the territories of the United States that were not yet states and the issue of states' rights generally.[29]

The Louisiana Purchase from France in 1803 greatly expanded the size of the United States. Totaling more than 800,000 square miles, it is the area occupied by the states of Arkansas, Missouri, Iowa, Minnesota west of the Mississippi River, North Dakota, South Dakota, Nebraska, Oklahoma, nearly all of Kansas, portions of Montana, Wyoming and Colorado east of the Rocky Mountains and Louisiana west of the Mississippi River, while also including New Orleans. James Monroe was one of the negotiators who met in France for its purchase on behalf of President Thomas Jefferson.[30]

This expansion of the United States created problems for statehood: keeping the balance between slave and free states. By the time Missouri and Maine had applied for statehood in 1820, the nation was bitterly divided over the issue of slavery. Henry Clay, then Speaker of the House of Representatives, was instrumental in striking a compromise—Missouri would be admitted as a slave state and Maine would be admitted as a free state, thus keeping a balance. Known as the Missouri Compromise, it also proposed that slavery be prohibited in the remainder of the Louisiana Purchase territory above the thirty-six-degree, thirty-minute latitude line. This provision held for thirty-four years until it was repealed by the Kansas-Nebraska Act of 1854. In 1857, the Supreme Court ruled that the Missouri Compromise was unconstitutional when it ruled in its *Dred Scott v. Sandford* decision.[31]

The Dred Scott case came before the Supreme Court in 1857. It involved determination of the constitutionality of the Missouri Compromise and the legal right of an enslaved man to become a citizen of the United States. Scott had been owned by an army surgeon, Dr. John Emerson of Missouri, who died in 1846. In 1836, Emerson took Scott to Fort Snelling in what is now Minnesota, a free territory that fell under the Missouri Compromise legislation. While there, Scott was given permission to marry a woman who was also a slave owned by Dr. Emerson. Eventually, Emerson returned to Missouri, taking Scott and his wife and their children with him. By 1846, Scott had apparently sought to buy his freedom, which was rejected. Scott then filed suit in the Missouri court on the grounds that his residence in the free territory of Minnesota released him from slavery. The Missouri Supreme Court ruled against him, writing that when Scott was brought back to Missouri, where slavery was legal, the enslaved status was reattached to him. Eventually, the case made its way to the U.S. Supreme Court. The case was argued in 1855 and 1856, with a final decision reached in 1857. The ruling, handed down by a majority vote, noted that there was no power existing in government to make citizens of Black people, slave or free, and that at the time of the formation of the Constitution they were not, and could not be, citizens of any of the states. The court ruled that Scott was still a slave and not a citizen of Missouri and that he had no right to sue in the federal court.[32]

Surprisingly, a Fugitive Slave Act was originally passed by Congress as early as 1793 providing for the seizure and return of runaway slaves. The act met with strong opposition in the North. As early as 1810, organized assistance was being offered to escaped slaves via the Underground Railroad. Demand from the South for more effective legislation resulted in the enactment of a second Fugitive Slave Act in 1850. Heavy penalties were imposed on federal marshals who refused to enforce the law, and penalties were imposed on individuals who helped slaves escape. Special commissioners were given jurisdiction with federal courts in enforcing the law. The result of this newly enacted act was that the number of abolitionists increased, the Underground Railroad became even more efficient and new personal liberty laws were enacted in many northern states.[33]

ABOLITIONISTS

The term *abolitionist* was commonly used in the United States from about 1835 until the close of the Civil War in 1865.[34] There were differences in the views of those who were cast into this group. Some were moderate in their views, calling for an immediate end to slavery, while the most extreme abolitionists outright refused to obey the Fugitive Slave Act or any section of the Constitution on which it was based. The more extreme abolitionists, responsible for operating the Underground Railroad, were transporting slaves to Canada. The moderates who called for an end to slavery also believed that if it were impossible, the North and South should go their separate ways. The extremist abolitionists believed that armed rebellion by slaves was the quickest way to end slavery.

"The practice of slavery is one of humankind's most deeply rooted institutions. Anthropologists find evidence of it in nearly every continent and culture dating back to ancient times and even the Neolithic period of human development. In Europe, the first significant efforts to ban human trafficking and abolish forced labor emerged in the 18th century."[35]

The history of Pennsylvania shows that slavery was, in fact, practiced in the early years of the colony. But religious influences as well as the cultural norms of some of Pennsylvania's earliest settlers brought about change over a period of time. While some Quakers in the early years owned slaves, a movement against slavery among the Friends began before Philadelphia was founded in 1682. Further, in 1688, a year that is remembered for the first formal protest against slavery in North America, the people of Germantown, which had been settled by German refugees, were stunned to find the existence of slavery. Simpleminded and honest men, they had no previous acquaintance with slavery.[36] Many Methodists and Presbyterians in Pennsylvania, like their Quaker neighbors, were opposed to slavery.

In 1780, Pennsylvania passed the Act for the Gradual Abolition of Slavery, which established certain steps in a process to end slavery. In 1847, the Pennsylvania legislature officially ended slavery.[37] The enactment of the 1850 Fugitive Slave Act, then, was a conundrum for the people of the Commonwealth. Those abolitionists who opposed slavery and took an active role in assisting fugitive slaves would now be in violation of this newly enacted federal law concerning fugitive slaves. The act and its ramifications were widely discussed in newspapers throughout the Commonwealth, with many posting a synopsis of the bill, notably how the bill applied to citizens, as well as marshals and their deputies: "4. Persons hindering the execution of the law to be fined $500 and imprisoned six months, and on conviction by trial of having caused the escape of a fugitive, to be fined $1,000 subject to recovery by law….8. It is provided that when a marshal or his deputies permit the escape of a fugitive from their possession, they shall be amenable to the value of the slave; and for default of duty in his capture, amenable to a fine of $1,000."[38]

As one "Political Preacher" put it, "'Thou shalt not return unto his master, the servant that is escaped from his master unto thee; he shall dwell with thee in one of thy gates, where it liketh him best,' This is God's Fugitive Slave law, but our Fugitive law says: Thou shalt return the slave or be fined and confined as the penalty. To preach the plain teaching of the above passage would condemn our national Fugitive Slave law. But to condemn this law is to preach politics. What shall this minister do in this case? Shall he stand up for God's law or man's law?"[39]

KNIGHTS OF THE GOLDEN CIRCLE (COPPERHEADS)

A notice in the *Brookville Republican* published on April 6, 1864, led to uncovering interesting information on a group that opposed the Civil War, the Knights of the Golden Circle, sometimes known as the Copperheads.

The heading on the article "Mystery Solved" described a strange jewel that was found on the steps of the post office:

It was evidently intended to be worn as a gentleman's breast pin, but was so strangely fashioned that its design could not be fathomed by those to whom it was shown. The principal part of the ornament was a golden ring or circle, the inner edge of which was covered with jet enamel, but coiled behind the ring was a tiny golden serpent, bright and glittering with two infinitesimal diamonds set at its head for eyes. It was beautifully wrought, and as a work of art, seemed to stand by itself, beyond praise, but its hidden signification was too much for the inquisitorial powers of all our hierarchs. What could it mean?[40]

The Knights of the Golden Circle was a secret society organized in the South in 1855 to promote slavery. One of its goals was to expand slavery into northern Mexico and into northern states. During the Civil War, Northern state members were advocating for a reduction in the powers of the federal government. In 1864, its membership peaked, reaching an estimated 200,000 to 300,000 members. Some Knights interfered with the Union war effort by hindering enlistments in the Union army and encouraging desertions. In 1864, with Union victory near, the society dissolved after a failed attempt to free Confederate prisoners in Illinois and Ohio and strong opposition by Northern governors.[41]

The *Raftsman's Journal*, published in Clearfield, Pennsylvania, carried a news story on April 18, 1860, about the Knights of the Golden Circle, noting that the organization

is attracting considerable attention, and a variety of rumors in regard to it are in circulation. We have little doubt that its strength and real importance are much exaggerated by the descriptions, which, in many cases, have their origin simply in a desire to excite curiosity and to win for it new recruits.... The current reports allege that the K.G.C. number forty thousand men, scattered throughout the southern states, who are well drilled and capable of furnishing, at short notice, an army twenty thousand strong...Its original design was to cultivate a martial spirit among the young men...within the last year or two its leaders have adopted new plans, and these have given it an impetus by which it has rapidly spread through all the Southern States, but more especially in Tennessee, Mississippi, Louisiana and Texas. Its object now is to get a foothold in Mexico, crush the Miramon faction [Miguel

Miramón, conservative Mexican president] *by cooperating with the Juarez Government, and then, as far as possible, Americanize the country, make it an outlet for slavery, and prepare it for the establishment of that institution.*[42]

The same newspaper, in 1862, printed an article, "Can It Be?," noting that the *Pittsburgh Dispatch* carried a story claiming that "a gentleman of our acquaintance asserts that there are about five hundred Knights of the Golden Circle in this county. We are loath to believe that such a number of men abide, even in Western Pennsylvania, so base as to have taken a solemn oath to disrupt this government. If there be any let them be exposed, in order that they may be properly dealt with."[43]

The aforementioned jeweled breast pin containing a tiny golden serpent gave rise to the common nickname in the Wilds region, Copperheads. There were many articles posted in area newspapers about their anti-Union activities. Soldiers wrote of their disdain for them. One newspaper asked the question, "What is the reason that when every Union-loving citizen is rejoicing over the victories gained by our brave armies, every Copperhead face has a look of gloom and sorrow?"[44]

A newspaper in Tioga County, Pennsylvania, occasionally ran an article titled "Select Poetry." One such poem, "Where Are the Copperheads," reveals the scorn that was felt by citizens of the region, with two stanzas reprinted here:

Go, look, upon the battle-field
    Where shot and shell fly fast,
Where Freedom's stirring battle-cry
    Is heard upon the blast.
Go where the lifted sabers flash
    And fall on traitor crests,
Where Southern bayonets are dim
    With blood from Northern breasts;
Go search amid the loyal ranks—
    Among the glorious dead;
Among them all you will not find a single Copperhead!

Go search the crowded hospital,
    Where ghastly wounds are seen,
Which tell through what a struggle fierce

These noble men have been;
But look upon their faces; lo!
They smile through all their pain;
The scars they have were nobly won—
Their honor has no stain;
Soft hands are ministering, kind words
Are heard around each bed,
Some soothe, some suffer—all are true;
There is no Copperhead![45]

"THE WAR COMMENCED"

There is a specific spirit in the people of the Wilds, a spirit that lingers from the days of the early settlers. The citizens of the Wilds are law-abiding, independent people who are able to take care of their own needs and make and assume responsibility for their decisions. The people of the Wilds are patriotic and put country first.

One headline in a local newspaper, "The War Commenced," gave the grim news of the fall of Fort Sumter:

We have the sad intelligence to communicate to our readers, that the long looked for collision between the Southern troops concentrated around Charleston harbor and the United States forces in Fort Sumter has taken place, and the garrison forced to surrender. The humiliating spectacle of the Stars and Stripes, being hauled down to be replaced by the rebel flag of South Carolina, upon public property, is a certain indication that a state of civil war now exists. One portion of the country is in open rebellion against the general government, and the prosperity [propensity] of a bloody war is now before us. Without waiting to argue the causes which have produced this sad state of affairs, it is our duty, as well as that of every American citizen, to stand by the government, and if necessary, defend the honor of our country's flag. The Southern States, although having just cause to lament the success of a sectional party, have carried their indignation too far, and having placed themselves in the position of open rebellion to the laws, and in a hostile position against the government, must bear the consequences of their own folly. If it could be a war between the fire-eaters of the South and the abolitionists of the North alone, we could look quietly on and rejoice at the extermination of both armies—but such cannot be now—matters have arrived at such a point that the true Union loving men are compelled to step forward and save the country. We give the latest news we have received, and will continue to keep our readers posted up on what is going on during the conflict. It is our opinion there will be a cessation of hostilities for the present, perhaps until after the meeting of Congress, during which time both parties will be preparing for a bloody conflict.[46]

Another paper ran what appeared to be a recruitment advertisement:

THE WAR BEGUN
Bombardment of Fort Sumter.
16 HOURS' FIGHTING.

THE UNCONDITIONAL SURRENDER
OF FORT SUMTER FULLY CONFIRMED

The President Calls for 75,000 Militia

Message from Gov. Curtin[47]

The War of 1812 highlighted the vulnerability of U.S. coastlines and harbors to attack from foreign countries. Construction of Fort Sumter was begun in 1829 and was still in progress in 1861. Situated on an artificial island at the entrance to Charleston Harbor, South Carolina, it was designed as part of a defensive system to protect the city.

By early 1861, the first seven of the eleven states to secede had left the Union: South Carolina, Mississippi, Florida, Alabama, Georgia, Louisiana and Texas. They claimed possession of all U.S. forts and arsenals within their territories. Two forts remained under federal jurisdiction: Fort Pickens in Florida and Fort Sumter. While troops were garrisoned at Sumter, it was of no strategic value to the Union, as its guns were pointed out to sea and the fort was incomplete. But it was a symbol of national union.[48]

When Lincoln took office in March, the Confederates demanded evacuation of the fort. The Confederates had erected other fortifications in the area, and Lincoln was faced with a decision to attempt to resupply the fort, which was in danger of being starved out, or abandon it. He prepared relief expeditions to both forts. Before the arrival of supplies, the Confederates demanded Fort Sumter's immediate evacuation. Major Robert Anderson, in command of the fort, refused to evacuate. The Confederates opened fire at 4:27 a.m. on April 12. By the afternoon of the thirteenth, Anderson had agreed to surrender, and his troops evacuated the fort at noon on April 14.[49]

Part II

WHAT WOULD I HAVE DONE?

Over 350,000 Pennsylvanians served in the Union Army,
more than any other Northern state except for New York. [50]

In researching certain eras in history where people exhibited extraordinary valor, who hasn't asked the question, "What would I have done?" Faced with rebellion within the country that led to secession and shots fired at Fort Sumter, what did the ordinary citizens of the Wilds do? This chapter reveals how men from the area reacted to the news of war, not asking themselves, "What should I do?" but rather, taking action.

THE BUCKTAIL REGIMENT

There is a monument in Driftwood, Cameron County, Pennsylvania, placed in 1908 and dedicated to the group known in the Civil War as the Bucktail Regiment. The inscription on the front of the marker reads, "This Monument at the instance of the people of Cameron County was erected by The State of Pennsylvania on April 17, 1908. Colonel Edward A. Irvin, Corporal Firmin E. Kirs, Sergeant William H. Raugh, commissioners." [51]

"Officially designated the 42nd Pennsylvania Volunteer Infantry, the unit was also known as the 12th Pennsylvania Reserves, the 1st Pennsylvania Rifle, the Kane Rifle and the 1st Bucktails. Due to the unique skill set of its soldiers, the regiment is often considered to be Pennsylvania's most famous Civil War

Above: Bucktail Monument, May 25, 2009. *Mike Wintermantel and www.hmdb.org.*

Left: The Bucktails Historic Marker, April 4, 2004. *Mike Wintermantel and www.hmdb.org.*

unit. In April 1861, a McKean County lawyer and abolitionist, Thomas L. Kane, was given specific instructions to assemble a company of riflemen from among the hardy woodsmen of McKean County. The recruiting was later expanded to Tioga, Cameron, Warren, Elk, Clearfield, Perry, Carbon and Chester Counties."[52]

While there were numerous fighting units from across the Wilds region, the Bucktails exhibited a spirit that is unique to the Wilds. A volunteer infantry regiment, they were woodsmen and lumbermen, experienced in the woods, could forage for themselves and, most importantly, were skilled marksmen.

Thomas L. Kane: Founder of the Bucktail Regiment

Kane, Pennsylvania, a community in the Wilds of McKean County, today known as the black cherry capital of the world,[53] takes its name from its founder.

Thomas Leiper Kane was not a person you would expect to find among the residents of the Wilds during the Civil War years, many of whom were the descendants of the rugged individuals who first set foot in the wilderness following the retreat of the Indians. Kane was born into a well-to-do family in Philadelphia.

Kane "had a broad range of interests.... Among his many humanitarian causes, Kane championed the end of the death penalty, peace, women's rights, the establishment of inner-city schools for young children, the abolition of slavery and liberty for religious

Thomas L. Kane. *From J.H. Beers & Company's* History of the Counties of McKean, Elk, and Forest, Pennsylvania *(1890).*

minorities. Besides being a reformer, Kane worked as a law clerk, a lawyer, a Civil War general, and a large-scale land developer...a cosmopolitan gentleman who spent his last twenty-five years in the rustic Alleghenies."[54]

His father, John Kintzing Kane, was an attorney, admitted to the bar on April 8, 1817. Eventually, John Kane became a member of the Pennsylvania legislature, a city solicitor and attorney general of Pennsylvania. Appointed a U.S. District Court judge, Kane was also a member of the first board of trustees at Girard College and president of the American Philosophical Society and was a promoter of the Academy of Fine Arts and Musical Fund

Society. Judge Kane was also connected with the Sunbury and Erie Railroad and the Chesapeake and Delaware Canal.[55]

Thomas Kane's mother, Jane Duval Leiper, came from a politically powerful family. Kane's famous brother, Elisha Kent Kane, an Arctic explorer who twice made his way to the far north, was regarded as a national hero.[56]

Thomas Kane remained in Philadelphia in his early life, eventually becoming a clerk in the Philadelphia District Court while his father was a federal judge.[57]

Kane's world vision changed, however, when he took a trip to Europe for health reasons in 1840. During this European excursion, he acquired a greater appreciation for America's freedoms.[58]

Returning to America in 1844, Kane was in Utah in 1846 visiting Mormon camps and crusading for their religious liberty. By December 1846, he was trying for an army commission in the Mexican-American War. His father wrote to Thomas's brother, Elisha, "Would you ever believe it, your philanthropist-philosopher-anti-war-anti-capital punishment brother, who denies the right of man to take life even for crime, Tom, even Tom Kane, is rabid for a chance of shooting Mexicans."[59]

Kane was about twenty-eight years old when the Fugitive Slave Act was enacted in 1850, an act that his father, as a federal judge, was sworn to uphold. The two clashed over the enforcement of the act, and Thomas, the abolitionist, became a participant in the Underground Railroad, hiding slaves making their way through Philadelphia on the second floor of his father's stable. "Judge Kane felt that his son was not faithfully obeying the law. Finally, he had him held in contempt of court and thrown into prison."[60] "Fortunately for Thomas, an associate justice of the U.S. Supreme Court, Robert C. Grier, overruled Judge Kane's conviction."[61]

In 1853, Thomas Kane married his sixteen-year-old second cousin, Elizabeth Dennistoun Wood. He encouraged his new bride to "enroll in the pioneering Philadelphia-based Female Medical College of Pennsylvania 'to help the college by the influence of her social position.'"[62] In their early years of marriage Elizabeth assisted Thomas in his battles against Philadelphia's urban poverty, as he founded and financed a school for Philadelphia's poor children."[63]

In 1855, reformer Thomas Kane came to the upper Clarion to visit lands owned by his father. With a group of friends, they found quarters near Wilcox in Elk County. In 1856, Kane brought his wife, Elizabeth, to the Wilds. Spending eight months of the year in the wilderness before returning to Philadelphia, by 1859 Kane had selected a location for a home in what is present-day Kane, McKean County. Construction began in 1860, but before he had made much progress, the drums of war were sounding; he abandoned the project to rally the men who formed the famous Bucktail Regiment. Sadly, the cut stone that was to be used for the foundation was stolen.[64] Elizabeth remained in Philadelphia during Kane's time in the service.

With the attack on Fort Sumter, Kane wrote to Pennsylvania governor Curtin for permission to recruit a company of volunteer riflemen from among the hardy woodsmen of McKean County, which grew to include Elk, Cameron, Tioga, Warren, Clearfield, Perry, Carbon and Chester Counties.[65]

There are two versions of how this famous group gained its name. The most popular version follows:

Opposite the Court House, where Col. Kane had his headquarters [Smethport] was a butcher shop, and one day a recruit noticed a deer's hide hanging outside. Crossing the street, he pulled his pen knife, cut off the tail and stuck it in his cap. Upon his return to headquarters, Col. Kane noticed his headgear, seized upon the idea suggested and instantly announced that the force he was recruiting should be known as "Bucktails."[66] While modern-day accounts have reported the name of the recruit who pulled his knife to cut off the tail, he has been identified by survivors of the Bucktails as James Landregan, a member of the McKean County Rifles.[67] Kane was assisted in his recruiting efforts by William Blanchard.

By April 23 Col. Kane had succeeded in enlisting his McKean Rifles and on that day they marched 28 miles from Smethport to Cameron, where they were joined by the Cameron Rifles. The next day they tramped to Sinnemahoning where they were joined by the Elk Rifles. Combined, the three companies totaled three hundred fifteen men, rough, thoroughly schooled in woods lore, dead shots and game to the core. For three days the men worked building rafts. On April 27 they embarked on the Sinnemahoning at Driftwood and floated down to Keating, where the stream broadens into the Susquehanna. Down the river they drifted to Lock Haven. Here they moored their rafts and entrained for Harrisburg.[68] Mostly lumbermen, they came dressed in red flannel shirts, carrying their rifles, proudly displaying a bucktail in their hats.[69] Kane said, "It was not in my power to procure uniforms. But red flannel for shirts was obtainable in quantity at the country shops, and felt hats. Bucktails, too, lie about our cabins by the dozen. Each volunteer was made to mount one of them in imitation of my own, and was directed to have faith that he would one day be prouder of it than any ostrich plume."[70]

Left: Elizabeth Kane. *L. Tom Perry Special Collections, Harold B. Lee Library, Brigham Young University.*

Below: White-tail deer. *Wikipedia Commons.*

Kinzua Bridge State Park Skyway. *John Myers.*

Kane was commissioned colonel of the regiment. However, Kane insisted that another man, an experienced Mexican-American War soldier, be elected colonel in his place. Kane's men requested the regiment name be changed to the Kane Rifle Regiment.[71] Kane fought in many battles, received a serious wound to the face and was captured at Harrisonburg, Virginia, and eventually released. He rose through the ranks, eventually becoming a brigadier general. In 1863, while he was at Gettysburg, he fell ill, in part from the wound to his face that didn't heal properly. Another assumed command.

Thomas Kane and his wife were in constant communication via letters. In 1863, when it was clear that he could no longer remain in the military because of his health, Thomas turned his attention once again to building their home in the Pennsylvania Wilds:

> *It will not be much, my own, but it will be enough to teach your inferiors around you who is their true superior, who is the highest among them of all truly refined and accomplished and generous Christian ladies. We will have to live very simply, but we can afford to have those around us we love who are truly worthy of being loved; and we will have still to continue to*

Above: Thomas L. Kane Memorial Chapel. *National Register of Historic Places, Wikimedia Commons, by Pubdog, February 22, 2011.*

Left: Thomas L. Kane plaque. *Wikimedia Commons, by Pubdog, June 27, 2009.*

work, but I will have time to hear you read the good books, and watch you photographing and help to educate the darling children....One year will see us (D. V.) [Deo Volente, meaning God Willing[72]] owners of a farm of a thousand acres, within a mile of the confines of a large and thriving business village....[73]

Kane was responsible for designating the routes of the Philadelphia and Erie Railroad; the Pittsburgh and Western; the Ridgway and Clearfield; and the New York, Lake Erie and Western Coal Railroad. He was the builder of the first Kinzua Bridge,[74] at one time the highest railroad bridge in the world. He eventually owned more than 100,000 acres of timberland, which included oil and gas rights.[75]

In 1869, not forgotten by his former commander and friend, it was with great anticipation that Thomas Kane waited to greet President Grant and his son, Jesse, when they arrived in Kane on the Presidential Special at 8:15 a.m. Apparently, Grant and his son were there to spend some relaxing time fishing. They first traveled by carriage to Kane's summer home, where Mrs. Kane and other members of the family served cake and wine. Next, traveling by horseback, Kane took them to meet with a group of men at Rasselas, where Grant fished at a location on Straight Creek. Later, continuing on horseback to Wilcox, President Grant stopped at the farm of Louis Hesalem, a soldier he met in the Civil War. At Wilcox, they were served a dinner at the home of Alonzo Wilcox. When they arrived back in Kane later in the evening, a bonfire was burning in front of the Kane home, where a large group of townspeople had gathered. A fife and drum corps greeted him, and a small cannon was ready to give a presidential salute. This was a visit the people of Kane long remembered.[76]

Thomas L. Kane died at Philadelphia on December 26, 1883, and was buried in the family plot. His body was later reinterred at the Kane Memorial Chapel in Kane, Pennsylvania.

William T. Blanchard:
Railroad Construction Worker and Volunteer, McKean County Rifles

William T. Blanchard was born in Palmer, Massachusetts, on March 26, 1838. He attended the common schools and also spent some time in high school and an academy at Warren, Massachusetts. Leaving school to work for a relative in Boston, in 1860 he traveled to New York to work for another relative involved in the promotion and construction of the Bradford and Pittsburgh Railroad in northwestern Pennsylvania. It was during this time that Blanchard met Thomas L. Kane. At the outbreak of the war, construction of the railroad was halted. Blanchard, in New York on April 18, was moved by the news of Fort Sumter.[77] Along with James Welch of Bradford, McKean County, the men left for Bradford, arriving on the evening of the nineteenth. As the men departed the train, they found a crowd assembled at the station. The sheriff of McKean County was one of those in the crowd carrying a letter from Kane to Blanchard. Kane was asking for Blanchard's help to recruit men in McKean County. Blanchard accepted the task, establishing a headquarters in Bradford.[78] By April 21, he had recruited thirty-four men to travel with him to Smethport. There Blanchard learned that Frank Bell and Bruce Rice had collected twenty-two more men. With the groups united, McKean County counted sixty-seven men ready to serve.

Kane made Blanchard his secretary, and his days were spent sending and receiving dispatches. With three companies of men from sparsely settled districts where telegraph connections were rare, Kane could only keep in touch with his lieutenants by means of messengers on horseback.[79]

On the afternoon of April 22, Kane administered the government oath to those who had signed the muster roll. The next day, after a hearty breakfast, the men assembled in the courtroom of the McKean County Courthouse to receive their first military instructions. At 8:00 a.m., the men marched to the Bennett House, where speeches were made and they were declared the McKean County Rifles. At nine o'clock, the command "Forward march" was given, and the men headed across the mountains to Cameron County. There they met John Eldred and the Cameron County Rifles. On April 24, the two companies were joined by the Elk County Rifles, as well as a few men from Tioga County.[80]

Arriving in Harrisburg, Blanchard, who had been elected captain, and his men became Company I of the Bucktails.[81]

Blanchard was wounded in both legs on June 6, 1862, at Harrisonburg, Virginia. His wounds were severe enough to cause him to resign on December 1, 1862. By September 1863, he had entered the Veteran Reserve Corps with the rank of captain. Following the war, Blanchard was involved in business ventures, but by 1899, he was crippled, living in Kentucky.[82]

Thomas B. Winslow: Recruiter and Volunteer, Elk County Rifles

With authorization received from Governor Curtin to raise troops, Kane advertised for volunteers:

> *Marksmen Wanted! By authority of Governor Curtin a company will be formed this week of citizens of McKean and Elk counties who are prepared to take up arms immediately to support the Constitution of the United States and defend the Commonwealth of Pennsylvania. I am authorized to accept at once for service any man who will bring with him to my headquarters a Rifle which he knows how to use. Come forward Americans who are not degenerate from the spirit of 1776. Come forward in time to save the city of Washington from Capture—in time to save the flag of the Union there from being humbled as it has been at Fort Sumter.*
>
> *(Signed) Thomas L. Kane.*[83]

In recent years, the village of Benezette has gained fame throughout the Wilds region and beyond for the wild elk herd that roams the fields and forests surrounding the town. The Elk Country Visitor Center and one of the main elk viewing areas nearby are both located on Winslow Hill. Reuben Colburn Winslow is credited with founding and naming the town,[84] and his nephew, George Winslow, is credited with naming the farming region where many of his family members resided Winslow Hill.[85] The farming area of Winslow Hill at one time supported its own school and a Methodist church.[86]

Thomas Benton Winslow was one of those living a simple life on Winslow Hill at the dawn of the Civil War. Born in Pennsylvania in 1836, he was about twenty-five years old when the war broke out. Some insight into his life can be learned from a study of federal census records. The census of 1850 reveals that an almost fourteen-year-old Thomas was living in his parents' home along with two brothers and two sisters. He attended school. His father was a farmer, and a brother was a laborer. By 1860, he, his father and brother were living with his married brother. He was employed as a blacksmith.[87]

Thomas Winslow's ancestral makeup may have contributed to the man he was to become. A direct descendant of nine passengers on the *Mayflower* through his mother's line, he was also a direct descendant of three Patriots of the Revolutionary War: two grandfathers and one great-grandfather.[88]

Thomas B. Winslow. *Library of Congress.*

Once Thomas Kane had recruited men in McKean County, he traveled to Benezette. The recruiting posters had been distributed in the region, and excitement was in the air. Meeting in a tavern, Kane was joined by Reuben Colburn Winslow, the founder of Benezette, known to Kane through the lumbering business. Thomas Winslow joined his uncle, Cobe (short for Colburn), in the recruitment effort. This work earned Thomas election as captain of the group that became known as the Elk County Rifles.[89]

Thomas B. Winslow enlisted with the Elk County Rifles on April 21, 1861, and again on May 15, 1861, as a private in the newly formed Company G, 42nd Pennsylvania Volunteer Infantry, 13th Pennsylvania Reserves. Winslow distinguished himself in his service and received a battlefield commission to first lieutenant on January 11, 1862. Wounded and captured at a battle near Harrisonburg, Virginia, on August 22, 1862, he was released on September 24, 1862.[90] Meeting up again with his unit in Maryland, he was at the Battle of Fredericksburg on December 13, 1862, where he was wounded for the second time, which put him out of action for more than a month. Having commanded Company K during the battle, he was assigned to that post from October 31, 1862, until February 28, 1863. In June 1863, he was assigned to perform recruiting duty at Clearfield, Pennsylvania, and also served as recruiter in Washington, D.C., and Harrisburg. He mustered out with the regiment on June 11, 1864.[91]

The year 1870 found him working as a stonemason in Jefferson County, Pennsylvania.[92] By 1873, an unmarried Thomas was a liquor dealer.[93] While no obituary or record of Thomas's death has been located, he died at the age of forty in 1876. This suggests that his wounds eventually took a toll on his life. Thomas B. Winslow is buried at Mount Pleasant Cemetery on Winslow Hill in Benezette.

Apparently, he was admired by the men in the "Valley," a region of Pennsylvania that extends from Benezette to Penfield, as in July 1882 an effort to establish a Grand Army of the Republic post in Penfield began. Organized by George Williams and Dr. J.H. Kline, a Civil War veteran, a charter was granted for the T.B. Winslow GAR Post No. 266. Starting with seventeen charter members, it soon grew to fifty-five members. The post also owned real estate.[94]

John A. Eldred:
Cameron County Sheriff and Volunteer, Cameron County Rifles

Another Bucktail Gone. Eldred—Died at Goldwin, Virginia, October 28th, 1905, in his eighty-first year, Captain John A. Eldred.[95]

Mr. Eldred was noted for his genial humor and delightful personality.[96]

As word of the bombing of Fort Sumter spread throughout the Wilds, the people of Cameron County were cognizant of Thomas Kane's efforts to recruit troops. A meeting was held at Emporium on April 20, 1861, organized by prominent men of the newly created Cameron County. The confidence the citizens expressed in Kane resulted in five resolutions regarding the question of war.

One of the participants in the war meeting was E.B. Eldred, who had been elected district attorney in 1860. Ironically, his younger brother, John A. Eldred, had been elected sheriff of Cameron County that same year.[97]

John Eldred was born in Milford, Pike County, Pennsylvania, in 1825. His parents were Richard and Harriet Baldwin Eldred.[98] His father was a lawyer, and like so many of Pennsylvania's early settlers, he had served his country during the War of 1812.

Sinnemahoning Creek, where three regiments of Bucktails began their journey by raft. *Nicholas A., Flickr.com.*

Arriving in Cameron County around 1850, John Eldred made his home with his brother, E.B. Eldred. Both were involved in lumbering.[99] In the 1860 federal census for Cameron County, Eldred's occupation was listed as storekeeper, this prior to his election as sheriff.

While John Eldred's personality, described in his obituary, paints him as a friendly man, he must have also exhibited natural leadership skills that resulted in his election as the first sheriff of Cameron County and that very possibly contributed to his appointment as this group's captain.

The first men to volunteer have been referred to as "Cameron County Company Old Bucktails."[100] In keeping with the theme of rugged woodsmen, Eldred's group was "noted for the size of its men as well as their prowess."[101]

Ready for the field by April 15, they joined with the McKean Rifles and the Elk County Rifles for a total of 315 men.[102] Gathering at a rafting place on the Sinnemahoning, the men began building rafts for transportation down the river: "Four rafts were constructed of rough pine board, sixteen feet long by ten inches or twelve inches wide by seven eighth inch thick. Each raft was composed of six platforms, each about sixteen feet square, made of six layers of boards laid crosswise and fastened together, making the dimensions of each raft about sixty-five feet by sixteen feet. On one of the rafts the thickness of one of the platforms was increased to seven layers, and on this platform Colonel Kane's horse, 'Old Glencoe' was placed. At one end of each of the rafts a large sweep or rudder was also constructed to assist the steersman in guiding the raft."[103]

After two days of work, on April 27, the three groups mounted the rafts, one carrying a green hickory pole with a bucktail attached for a flagstaff and the Stars and Stripes flying high. With the strains of fife and drums echoing through the forest, they began their journey to Harrisburg.[104]

Eldred led his men until September 10, 1861, when he resigned. He was replaced by L.W. Gifford, who was promoted from second lieutenant and served as Eldred's successor until November 17, 1862.[105]

Eventually, Eldred left Cameron County for business interests in the far West. About ten years before his death, he settled in Virginia near two of his brothers. There is no record that he was ever married.

THE DRAFT

HE VOTED FOR THE DRAFT. BY ONE WHO WAS TAKEN IN

"Good people vote for Abe,
*   The Union to restore,*
To liberate the negro
*   And end this cruel war.*
We'll have no more conscription,"
*   Said the Lincoln men and laughed,*
"So vote for Abraham
*   If you'd avoid the draft"*

"As soon as rebeldom
*   Shall hear the glorious news,*
Of Abraham's election,
*   They'll tremble in their shoes,*
They'll throw away their arms,"
*   Said the Lincoln men and laughed;*
"So vote for Father Abraham
*   If you'd avoid the draft."*

"Jeff Davis and Bob Lee
*   Will go to Mexico,*
And Beauregard and Hood will hide
*   Themselves in Borneo.*
They'll give us their plantations,"
*   Said the Lincoln men and laughed,*
"So vote for Father Abraham,
*   If you'd avoid the draft."*

I took them at their word,
I voted for their man,
And sat up all election night,
*   To hear how Shoddy ran,*
The telegraph did tick,
*   The Lincoln men all laughed,*
And said, "the Copperheads are sick,
*   There'll be another draft!"*

No copperhead am I,
But still I feel quite sick,
*   To think the draft should follow*
My vote for Abe so quick,
I asked the Democrats,
*   How is this? and they laughed,*
*   And said, "How are you conscript,*
*   YOU VOTED FOR THE DRAFT!"*[106]

For the first time in U.S. history, Congress passed a conscription act in 1863, known to the average person as the draft. The act was to register all males between the ages of twenty and forty-five, including aliens who intended to become citizens by April 1 of that year. Although the Civil War saw the first compulsory conscription of males for service, there were other instances where the government dictated terms to the population. By an act of Congress in 1792, all able-bodied male citizens were required to purchase a gun and join a local militia. However, there was no penalty for noncompliance. During the War of 1812, Congress passed a conscription act, but the war ended before it could be enacted.[107]

The draft was not popular among the people, particularly those of the working or lower class. For those who could afford it, exemptions could be purchased for $300 or by finding a substitute draftee. Because of this practice, the troops were made up of those who volunteered or those who were drafted, whether or not the draftee wanted to serve.[108]

Civil War draft wheel. *National Museum of American History.*

In Warren County, large numbers of men volunteered for service at the news of Fort Sumter. It was estimated that by 1862, 1,154 men had been sent into the field from Warren County for Pennsylvania regiments and 166 for New York regiments. The county commissioners in that year appropriated a bounty payment of $1,000 to encourage enlistment to meet quotas. Things changed when the draft was instituted. By 1864, some men in Warren County were questioning whether they were willing to serve. Left with one alternative, to pay for substitutes, many turned to the county for "bonding,"[109] a system where county monies were used for the purpose of paying substitutes. This was considered unfair by those soldiers who had willingly gone to war, only to return home to help pay for those who didn't want to go.

Bloody Knox, Clearfield County

After the Battle of Gettysburg, resistance occurred in New York City in what was known as the New York City Draft Riots of 1863. By August 1864, Clearfield County had a 600-man draft list. With resentment growing against the draft, only 150 men responded to the call.[110]

In June 1863, Assistant Marshal David Cathcart was shot in Knox Township by draft dodgers working as loggers. "Homes were set on fire in Graham Township by draft dodgers while deserters were looting throughout the county. Copperheads liberated arrested deserters in Troutville and secret societies were formed to resist the draft and gather slaves. In October, 1864, recruitment officer, Col. Cyrus Butler was killed in Lawrence Township by draft deserter Joseph Lounsberry. Afterwards, the government sent troops to county."[111]

Bloody Knox. *www.visitclearfieldcounty.org*

In 1861, Tom Adams, his wife and two children were living in Knox Township in a log cabin he built in Kellytown. Having enlisted in the army in 1862, Adams became a deserter from the 149th Bucktails in 1863 and returned to his home. Because of the resistance in Clearfield County, federal troops were deployed to Philipsburg under the direction of a Captain Southworth. Acting on a tip that a party was being held at Adams's cabin, in December 1864, troops surrounded the structure, calling for the surrender of the deserters and draft dodgers inside. Adams shot a soldier from New Hampshire, and shots were fired in return, killing Adams in his yard. The troops arrested 18 men that night, with another 150 being arrested within a month. The Civil War ended four months later.

In the fall, a reenactment takes place at the Bloody Knox cabin once owned by Tom Adams in Clearfield County.

WOMEN IN THE WAR

Clara Barton: A Self-Taught Nurse

Clara Barton. *Library of Congress.*

Most people recognize the name Clara Barton for her work with the American Red Cross. Born Clarissa Harlowe Barton on December 25, 1821, in Massachusetts, she died in Glen Echo, Maryland, on April 12, 1912. She is also known for her work in the American Civil War at a time when there was no formal nursing education. Clara was self-taught.

Having worked in education in Canada and Georgia, Barton moved to Washington, D.C., in 1855 to work at the U.S. Patent Office, where she received a salary equal to that of a man, which was opposed by the male clerks. Eventually, her position was reduced, and in 1858, under the administration of James Buchanan, she was fired because of her "Black Republicanism." Living with relatives in Massachusetts for three years, after the election of Abraham Lincoln she returned to the patent office as a temporary copyist.[112]

On April 19, 1861, the week after Fort Sumter, the Baltimore Riot resulted in the first bloodshed of American troops. Victims in the Massachusetts regiment were transported by train to Washington, D.C. Barton went to the railroad station with the thought of serving her country by providing assistance. Upon arrival, she recognized many of the men she had grown up with. That day was a turning point for her. They were wounded and short on clothing, food and supplies. Barton determined to help them. In spite of opposition from the War Department and field surgeons, she quickly learned how to store and distribute medical supplies. With a few friends, Barton formed the Ladies' Aid Society for the distribution of bandages, food and clothing to the wounded. In 1862, she gained permission to work on the front lines. Known as the "Florence Nightingale of America," she assisted troops at the Battles of Fairfax Station, Chantilly, Harpers Ferry, South Mountain, Antietam, Fredericksburg, Charleston, Petersburg and Cold Harbor.[113]

Searching the histories of the counties that today make up the Pennsylvania Wilds, few references are made to the nurses in those military histories. Following are three examples of women who served as nurses, one woman from Jefferson County, one from Elk County and one from Clinton County. The latter two became nurses simply because they followed their husbands to war.

Kate Scott, Brookville, Pennsylvania

Kate Scott was a remarkable woman in the annals of Jefferson County history. She was born in Ebensburg, Cambria County, Pennsylvania, on October 5, 1837, and her parents soon relocated to Brookville, Jefferson County, where she spent her childhood years. Her father was a printer who published the *Brookville Republican*, with which she assisted him while learning the publishing business. In later years, she wrote two histories, one about Jefferson County and the other about the military unit raised in the area, the 105th Pennsylvania Regiment, the Wildcats.[114]

Kate was dating a young man from Clarion County in the time leading up to the Civil War, and once hostilities broke out at Fort Sumter, he, as with other men in the region pushed by the fervor of preserving the Union, signed up to join the fight. Not wanting him to go, Kate determined that she would go with him as a nurse. Reaching out to the commander of the military district where her friend had gone, within several weeks she received

The *Brookville Republican* was started in 1850 by John Scott, father of Kate Scott, and was later owned by J.R. Weaver. *From* Caldwell's Atlas of Jefferson County, Pennsylvania *(1878)*.

instructions on how to apply. "The requirements read that only those women who were of temperate habits, plain of sight, buxom but restrained in their relations to others, and impeccable morals need apply."[115]

Making application, she received authorization to report to Colonel McKnight at Camp Jameson near Alexandria, Virginia. Her instructions included a stop at Harrisburg to draw money for the trip to Washington. Arriving at the state capital, no one knew anything about her orders or the travel money. She stayed in a boardinghouse with other young women and took a job sewing uniforms. Saving all that she could, when she finally reached sixteen dollars, the amount she had been promised for travel, she made a train trip to Washington on her own. Arriving in January, the provost marshal did not recognize Kate's orders, noting that no woman could pass over the river to Virginia. Eventually, through her sheer determination, disguised as a man, she walked to Camp Jameson, where she made contact with Colonel McKnight. After he recognized her as the person he knew in

Brookville, she was put to work as a nurse. Arriving when an epidemic had been raging for several weeks, she worked every day, sixteen to twenty hours per day. The hospital was a clapboard building, with snow blowing through the floor and walls. Some of the sick were housed in tents, requiring the nurses to wade through heavy snow to get from one tent to another. Some of the officers were not respectful of the women.[116]

By the first of March, Kate had moved to a boardinghouse in Washington where several girls she worked with were living. Colonel McKnight offered her the opportunity to go south with the regiment. After careful consideration, she decided to return to Brookville in June.

In her own words, Kate wrote:

> *In December, 1861, in response to a call from the officers of the One Hundred and Fifth Regiment Pennsylvania Volunteers, for persons to volunteer to nurse the sick of that regiment, the writer* [Kate] *in company with Misses Ellen Guffey, Mary G. Fryer, and Mary P. Allen, joined the regiment at Camp Jameson, Virginia, and were enrolled as regimental nurses, where we did what lay in our power to aid the recovery of the many who were stricken down by disease; and, as far as in us lay, to soothe and comfort those who, letting go of life, went upon the long march that ended in the grave. With their cold hands in ours, their dying voices breathing loving messages to the dear ones at home, we saw them go down into the cold valley, one by one. It seemed terrible to us then, that they, so young, so buoyant, should die; but we know now that they, in obeying the call of the Great Captain who ordered them to his headquarters, were only the "advance guard" of the many who swelled the "death-roll" of our brave old regiment. Brave, noble boys, though you died in the hospital, ere you had "broken lance" with the enemy, you died none the less for your country, than did those of your comrades who went down in the storm of battle. We remained with the regiment until the eve of their departure for the Peninsula, when, no provision being made for nurses, we returned home.*[117]

In addition to writing the two histories mentioned earlier, Kate was postmaster of Brookville for four years, having been appointed in the summer of 1890 by President Harrison. She was secretary of the National Association of Army Nurses, which met annually with the National GAR Encampment.[118] Kate was a member of the Women's Relief Corps, an organization of patriotic women, auxiliary to the Grand Army of the Republic, and she and Annie Wittenmyer pushed for the establishment

The Pennsylvania Memorial Home was housed in the Philip Taylor House, Brookville. *National Register of Historic Places, Wikimedia Commons.*

of the Pennsylvania Memorial Home in Brookville, which was housed in the Philip Taylor House. The first of its kind in the nation, it provided a home for former soldiers, wives, children, widows and orphans.[119] The WRC organization exists to this day and recently joined with Penn Highlands Health Care System.

Kate never married and died in her beloved Brookville on April 15, 1911.

Sarah Ellen Miller Caldwell Johnson, Ridgway, Pennsylvania

Sarah Ellen Miller was the daughter of James and Hannah Rose Miller and was born in Mercer County, Pennsylvania, in 1843.[120] At the age of nineteen, on January 9, 1862, she married Robert Caldwell the same day he left for the war. As did many other women, Sarah followed him into service and ended up in Alexandria, Virginia, where she worked in an emergency hospital. Given charge, she was there when her wounded husband was brought in for care. He died in that same hospital on November 12, 1862. Sarah continued to be in charge of the hospital until the close of the war.[121] One can speculate that she was a strong and capable individual to have been given the position she held for so long.

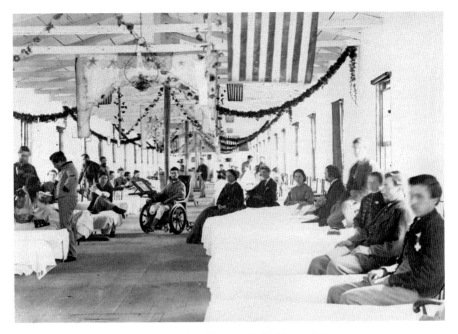

A ward in Armory Square Hospital, Washington, D.C. *Library of Congress.*

Even though Alexandria is located in Virginia, which was part of the Confederacy, the town was used as a base for supplies, troop transfer and other logistics by the Union army and as protection for Washington, D.C. By the end of the war, there were more than thirty military hospitals in Alexandria with 6,500 beds.[122]

While no written record has been found of Sarah's experiences as a Civil War nurse, the letter of a Quaker woman from New York State, Julia Wilbur, written on Christmas Eve 1862 provides a graphic description of the day's events:

> *You at a distance cannot image what a place this is at present. It was last Friday that 700 wounded were brought here. All day long the ambulances were busy in moving them from the boats to the hospitals. A great many slightly wounded were able to walk & will soon be well. In one hospital I saw one ward filled up. Their wounds had been well dressed & they said they were well cared [for], they have plenty of blankets & they were moved just as carefully as could be & laid on those clean white beds as tenderly as it could have been done at home....Among all these wounded, suffering men, I heard not a groan nor a complaint.[123]*

Sarah Miller Caldwell married again on September 9, 1865, to another who had been a Civil War soldier, Thomas B. Johnson. He had been a member of Company G of the Bucktails, having enlisted in Kane in 1861. He was wounded at the Battle of Gettysburg. The newlyweds lived briefly at Tidioute in Warren County and Hallton in Elk County before moving to Ridgway three years after the war. In spite of his wounds, Thomas lived for a number of years. He passed away in 1899, and a historian recorded that he died from the wounds inflicted those many years earlier.[124] Mother to sons Robert and Thomas, Sarah died at her home on West Main Street and is buried alongside her husband at Pine Grove Cemetery.[125]

Sarah Elizabeth Peese Boyer Simcox, Clinton County, Pennsylvania

A newspaper headline read, "She Was Civil War Nurse, Interesting Reflections of a Clinton County Woman." The article began:

> Youthful acquaintance of Ulysses S. Grant in the days before he was considered as the future great general; of James A. Beaver, when he too was but a youth, with his honors as Union General and Governor of Pennsylvania yet to come; but more than that, as a young wife, a woman with courage sufficient to send her hundreds of miles on her first railroad journey that she might reach the bedside of her husband, wounded in the Wilderness fight, only to have him later die a Confederate prisoner—that is the brief but thrilling history of Mrs. Sarah Elizabeth Simcox, now a woman of seventy-eight who resides in an ancient log home in a hollow bearing her name, six miles east of Lock Haven.[126]

The article appeared in a Tioga County newspaper in 1920. The writer described Sarah as an old lady with a face lined from age and eyes that were sad, except when she spoke about parts of her life's narrative.

She was born in Centre County the daughter of John and Lovey Ann Peese. Her father was a native of Switzerland, and her mother was the daughter of a man who was a great hunter. Sarah had six siblings, a large family. Close to her grandparents, Sarah often spent time at their home assisting her grandfather in skinning the game that he caught.

At sixteen, Sarah's life changed when Abram Boyer from Jefferson County, Pennsylvania, came to work as a farmhand at the local Curtin farm. In 1860, Sarah and Abram were married at Milesburg, Centre County, by a Methodist minister. With war on the horizon, it wasn't long after the marriage that Fort Sumter was attacked in April 1861, and Abram took Sarah back to her parents' home and enlisted for three months' service. At the end of his enlistment, he briefly returned to Sarah, but with the war still raging, he reenlisted for three years in the Bald Eagle Infantry. On September 12, 1861, the local infantry left for Washington, D.C., where it became Company A, 45th Pennsylvania Volunteers. Before the ninety-five men who were bound for war left their homes, the wives, mothers, sisters and sweethearts prepared a dinner at Howard. At the train station on the day of their departure, flags were flying, and a band played as the train moved away with its passengers headed south.[127]

Following training, the company fought in battles at South Mountain, Antietam, Blue Springs and Crab Orchard. Abram wrote occasionally during the next nineteen months, but there were no furloughs home. Sarah received word that Abram had been wounded at the Battle of the Wilderness on May 6, 1864, and she was determined to be with him. Boarding a train for the first time in her life, it was a two-day trip from Milesburg to Annapolis. Arriving at a hotel, she found that it was full, with General Grant and his family among other guests. Sarah had known Grant when he was young, having met him at Bellefonte during one summer vacation. Sarah found other accommodations.

After she called on General Grant, he assisted her in locating her wounded husband by finding Lieutenant Waldo C. Vanvalin, who recognized Sarah from home. When asked what she was doing there, Sarah replied, "I just came down to see you fellows and to shoot a couple of Rebels!"[128] Eventually, Sarah was led to her husband. While it was reported that he was struck in the right shoulder by a rifle ball and a few minutes later by another ball entering his right leg at the hip, coming out on the inside near the knee, he was in remarkably good condition. Because he required surgery, he remained off duty to receive daily care.

At the hospital, another life-changing event occurred when she found two of her former Howard schoolmates, Adam Brade and George Brown, both wounded and badly in need of nursing care. Again, another woman who was not a trained nurse pitched in to provide care for the injured. Her husband found her lodging with a woman Sarah believed was a Rebel, as she often claimed that the soldiers should be killed and Washington should be burned. At the surgeon's request, Sarah remained for six weeks before making plans to return home. In appreciation for her service, the army surgeon provided her with ten dollars.

General S.P. Heintzelman and group, Convalescent Camp near Alexandria, Virginia. *Library of Congress.*

Abram Boyer returned to Centre County following his discharge but only for a few weeks. He enlisted a third time, going back to his old company, which was by then with the Army of the Potomac. Sarah once again followed him south a few weeks later and stayed there until General Grant told her that the army was about to move and that she could return when a new camp was set up. She left her husband on September 29, and Abram was captured by the Confederates the next day. A prisoner at Andersonville for a month, he died in Salisbury, North Carolina, on November 1, 1864. Sarah was told that her husband died on the floor of a shanty and that a member of Company D of his regiment, a man known to Sarah, became a Rebel when he was imprisoned by the Confederates, who made him a prison trusty. Abram begged the man to read from the Bible the passage that says, "In my Father's house are many mansions," but instead the turncoat kicked him. Abram died on the floor of that shanty. When the turncoat returned to Pennsylvania, a reward was offered for his apprehension, and he disappeared. Sarah said that she would have killed him if she ever met him.[129]

Sarah eventually married Samuel Simcox, a young lawyer, and the couple had two children, a boy and a girl. They settled in the log building in Simcox Hollow, the exact location where she gave the interview about her nursing experiences. Sarah Simcox died in 1932 at the age of eighty-nine.

Part III

NORTH STAR WAY

The Underground Railroad

I n 1967, Mrs. John Crowe of Johnstown won a contest to rename Route 219, 254 miles of roadway running from the Maryland border north to the New York State line, including through several counties in the Pennsylvania Wilds. Mrs. Crowe said that she selected her winning name, "North Star Way," because the highway goes north–south and the North Star serves as a guide to navigators and travelers.[130]

Historically, the name could apply to early settler roads and Indian paths pushing through northwestern Pennsylvania used by runaway slaves to reach Canada, their North Star destination. According to the National Park Service, "As slave lore tells it, the North Star played a key role in helping slaves to find their way—a beacon to true north and freedom. Escaping slaves could find it by locating the Big Dipper, a well-recognized asterism most visible in the night sky in late winter and spring. As the name implies, its shape resembles a dipping ladle, or drinking gourd. From the gourd's outline, the North Star could be found by extending a straight line five times the distance from the outermost star of the bowl."[131]

The "movement" to free slaves used railroad terminology to hide the purpose of what was taking place. "The term 'conductor' was used to describe the people who guided the fugitive slaves. Hiding places included private homes, churches and schoolhouses. These were called 'stations,' 'safe houses' and 'depots.' The people operating them were called 'stationmasters.'"[132]

Various methods were used by runaway slaves to make their escape, most traveling by foot, while others utilized specially designed wagons, traveled on railways in containers or by water in canoes and even coastal schooners.[133]

$200 Reward.

RANAWAY from the subscriber, on the night of Thursday, the 30th of Sepember,

FIVE NEGRO SLAVES,

To-wit: one Negro man, his wife, and three children.

The man is a black negro, full height, very erect, his face a little thin. He is about forty years of age, and calls himself *Washington Reed*, and is known by the name of Washington. He is probably well dressed, possibly takes with him an ivory headed cane, and is of good address. Several of his teeth are gone.

Mary, his wife, is about thirty years of age, a bright mulatto woman, and quite stout and strong.

The oldest of the children is a boy, of the name of FIELDING, twelve years of age, a dark mulatto, with heavy eyelids. He probably wore a new cloth cap.

MATILDA, the second child, is a girl, six years of age, rather a dark mulatto, but a bright and smart looking child.

MALCOLM, the youngest, is a boy, four years old, a lighter mulatto than the last, and about equally as bright. He probably also wore a cloth cap. If examined, he will be found to have a swelling at the navel.

Washington and Mary have lived at or near St. Louis, with the subscriber, for about 15 years.

It is supposed that they are making their way to Chicago, and that a white man accompanies them, that they will travel chiefly at night, and most probably in a covered wagon.

A reward of $150 will be paid for their apprehension, so that I can get them, if taken within one hundred miles of St. Louis, and $200 if taken beyond that, and secured so that I can get them, and other reasonable additional charges, if delivered to the subscriber, or to THOMAS ALLEN, Esq., at St. Louis, Mo. The above negroes, for the last few years, have been in possession of Thomas Allen, Esq., of St. Louis.

WM. RUSSELL.

ST. LOUIS, Oct. 1, 1847.

$200 reward for "Five Negro Slaves." *Library of Congress.*

One such escape route that passed through the Wilds was the Bedford to Clearfield route. Bedford was only twenty miles from the Maryland border, with the town of Cumberland serving as a major staging place for the Underground Railroad. The most popular route from Bedford was through Fishertown, a Quaker community. Following the old Conemaugh Indian path, the fugitives made their way through the Pigeon Hills, where the Quaker families assisted them. The next part of the journey took them to Clearfield in the Wilds region. Clearfield also had a strong Quaker presence, as well as 104 free Black residents. Once there, another leg of the journey went on to Brookville in Jefferson County, traveling over the Indian Venango-Chinklacamoose Path, which ran from Clearfield to Brookville. Brookville was an important stop along the Underground Railroad. There the fugitives were assisted by a group of Methodists.[134] Various routes were followed from Brookville, such as the Brookville to Franklin route and the Brookville to Warren route, which placed the slaves closer to the New York border.

UNDERGROUND STATIONS IN THE WILDS

As mentioned, people and locations within the Wilds were heavily involved in the Underground Railroad. The following sections focus on locations in each of the twelve and a half counties making up the Pennsylvania Wilds.

Cameron County, Pennsylvania

Cameron County, the least populated county in the state, was formed in March 1860 from parts of Clinton, Elk, McKean and Potter Counties. It was also on the central route of the Underground Railroad, with runaways coming from Maryland and Virginia following the Susquehanna River. Fugitives taking the central route through Pennsylvania arrived at Elmira, New York, eventually trekking on to Niagara and Canada.[135]

One of the escape routes through Cameron County originated in Williamsport, Lycoming County, to the east and through Lock Haven, Clinton County. Fugitives were guided from Williamsport over the Great Shamokin Path west along the banks of the West Branch of the Susquehanna River to Great Island near Lock Haven. Leaving Great Island and continuing along the banks of the West Branch of the Susquehanna near the Cameron-Clinton County line, the Sinnemahoning Path veered northward from the Great Shamokin Path.[136] This path provided access to "stations" in Potter and McKean Counties.

The name Sinnemahoning is a corruption of an Indian name, Achsinni-mahoni, or "Stoney Lick."[137] In the early days of Pennsylvania, the Sinnemahoning Path was used for settlers migrating into McKean, Potter and Clinton Counties. The path was said to provide the easiest grades across Pennsylvania's mountains and may well have been the path used by Indians thousands of years ago coming from the west into Pennsylvania.[138]

While the route provided an easier grade through the mountains, imagine the life of the fugitive slave traveling through the thick forests of Pennsylvania. For safety, fugitive slaves

Sinnemahoning Path, May 24, 2013. *Mike Wintermantel and www.hmdb.org*

traveled at night, fearful of encountering slavers during the daylight hours. They did not light fires to warm themselves, as this might draw attention to them. Without shelter, they endured wet weather, sometimes taking refuge in rock shelters utilized at an earlier time by the Indians. Without a steady supply of food, they were often hungry. Without friends, they were naturally suspicious of anyone they might come across who offered assistance.

In the words of one who made his escape with his wife in August 1849, "Rain had been falling all day. For a week it poured. We had no shelter nor a way to keep ourselves dry. During the day we rested as best we could under some thick tree or overhanging rocks, which sheltered us a little from the rain. At night we traveled….Alone either of us would have given up…although we were wet and hungry, and footsore, we never lost our determination. We knew that if we went back or were captured, we should be sold down the river."[139]

One stop on the Underground Station in Cameron County was at the home of William Lewis at Clear Creek.[140] Mr. Lewis was born in New Jersey in 1806, as was his wife, Sarah Chadwick, born in 1808. They were the parents of a large family. Both the Lewis and Chadwick families were early settlers in Cameron County. Sarah Chadwick was the daughter of a Revolutionary War Patriot Elihu Chadwick. There are no written accounts as to the extent of their involvement in the Underground Railroad, but their home at Clear Creek in the Rich Valley region outside Emporium surely provided a welcome relief to those traveling the Sinnemahoning Path on their way to freedom in Canada.

Sarah Chadwick Lewis had a brother, Elihu Chadwick Jr., who was a participant in the Underground Railroad in Venango County. As slaves traveled through Clarion County and into Venango County, Chadwick was there to receive them.

Chadwick had been sent to Rockland Township, Venango County, in the early years to survey land owned by the Bingham heirs mapping out farmlands for people migrating into Western Pennsylvania. While settling there with his wife and family, his farm served as a hiding place for fugitive slaves.

Described as a man who "was very dedicated to the cause of freedom and to the freeing of the negro slaves in the South,"[141] he hid them in "a large room or cellar constructed underground, near the huge barn. It was walled and ceiled with hand-picked stone, well fitted together to prevent cave-in."[142] It appears that the freeing of slaves was a Chadwick family attribute and involved a brother and sister living in two different locations.

(Northern) Centre County, Pennsylvania

Bellefonte in northern Centre County is known as the "Welcome Mat" of the Pennsylvania Wilds.[143] Bellefonte is an old community that was laid out in 1795 and named by Talleyrand for "beautiful fountain." It was the one-time home of five of Pennsylvania's governors. It was also active in the Underground Railroad.

Andrew Gregg Curtin was born in Bellefonte in 1817 to a Scotch-Irish immigrant iron founder and his wife, who was the daughter of a major politician and president pro tem of the U.S. Senate. Curtin's parents placed a high value on education. He was sent to preparatory school in Harrisburg and then to the academy at Milton.

In 1860, Curtin was part of a "People's Party," made up of Republicans, Whigs and Democrats who favored Republican policies but, in order to avoid war, were conservative on issues of slavery. He defeated his Democratic opponent by thirty thousand votes one month before Lincoln became president. Voters understood that regardless of favoring conservative issues on slavery, through his leadership Pennsylvania was on the side of the Union. Elected to a second term in 1863, through health issues and the logistics of having a state that fed the Union cause with massive units for the army, he was known as the "Soldier's Friend." Through his leadership, supplies, transport and support personnel were provided for the troops in the field. He was responsible for establishing the Soldiers' Orphan Schools following the war. Serving in various offices throughout the years, at retirement Curtin returned to his hometown of Bellefonte. When he died in 1894, he was honored as a hero and statesman by thousands, who paid their respects in his hometown. His funeral was escorted by military troops, who remembered his important role in the Civil War.[144]

Bellefonte had four stops on the Underground Railroad: the Linn House, St. Paul AME Church, William Thomas House and Samuel Harris House.

The article "Scholar Talks About Bellefonte's Underground Railroad Connection" in *The Express* by Emma Gosaloz describes a presentation by Dr. Donna King, a nationally known African American scholar, lecturer at Penn State University and pastor of St. Paul African Methodist Episcopal Church in Bellefonte. According to the article, there was an early antislavery movement in Centre County, with Bellefonte becoming a home for former slaves and freedmen. The movement revolved around churches in the community:

With its Quaker roots, Bellefonte has long been a place where people of different races and backgrounds could live and work side by side. From

Left: Andrew Gregg Curtin, Civil War governor of Pennsylvania. *Wikimedia Commons.*

Below: Henry S. Linn House, one of the Underground Railroad stops in Bellefonte. *Historic American Buildings Survey, Library of Congress.*

Mills Brothers group (1956), whose ancestors escaped slavery in the South via the Underground Railroad, settling in Bellefonte. *Wikimedia Commons.*

about 1818 until the Civil War, Bellefonte was a stop on the Underground Railroad and several homes, as well as St. Paul's AME Church in the town have now been identified as being former safe houses for runaway slaves. In the late 1820s, the ancestors of the famous Mills Brothers singing group escaped slavery in the South by the Underground Railroad. Upon arriving in Bellefonte, they decided to stay rather than continue on to Canada. Of their four sons, Lewis and Edward Mills joined the Union Army's Colored Troops and fought in the Civil War. Lewis' son, William Hutchinson Mills (b. 1847, d. 1931) was grandfather to the singing Mills Brothers.[145]

Clarion County, Pennsylvania

Clarion County is the western gateway to the Pennsylvania Great Outdoors and Pennsylvania Wilds regions.[146] Its history reveals that its citizens were greatly moved by the attack on Fort Sumter. On April 26, 1861, the local newspaper reported that a large, enthusiastic crowd attended a meeting on

April 22 at the Presbyterian church in Clarion, where a committee of nine had been formed to respond to the recent rebellion:

> *Whereas, Rebellious hands have been raised in armed violence against the legally constituted authorities of that Government, purchased with blood and framed by the wisdom of our Forefathers, Therefore,*
>
> *Resolved, That believing we truly represent the unanimous feelings of a people devoted in their loyalty to the Union and its government, we do hereby pledge ourselves without reservations, to the maintenance of that Union and Government, with all the means that "God and nature have placed in our power."*[147]

The committee went on to outline a series of actions to be taken, including gathering volunteers to join the military.

In addition to answering the call to arms, Clarion County also had an active Underground Railroad network that was functioning as early as June 1847. Five men—Reverend John Hindman of Armstrong County and William Blair, Reverend John McAuley, James Fulton and Benjamin Gardner Sr. of Clarion County—were the stationmasters responsible for conveying the fugitives through Clarion County. Hindman, McAuley and Fulton were members of the Seceder Church, with many of its congregation being active abolitionists.

On the western route of the Underground Railroad, Hindman received fugitive slaves in Dayton, Armstrong County, where he handed them off to the men in Clarion County and Blair of Porter Township, who sent them on to McAuley in Rimersburg. McAuley kept the fugitives in his barn until twilight or total darkness, when he and his son guided them to Fulton, who lived north of Rimersburg. The slaves told their stories to their guides. One fugitive, a large man of nearly six feet, three inches, with an estimated weight of 240 pounds, noted that when his master tried to whip him, because of his size, he would catch

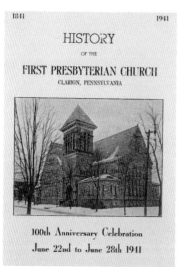

"History of the First Presbyterian Church, Clarion, Pennsylvania and the 100th Anniversary Celebrations, June 22nd to June 28th, 1941," by Wilson L. Theophilus (1941). *www. archives.org.*

his master and hold him, thereby escaping many whippings. Another slave recounted that he left his wife, believing that "if the Lord spared him," he would return one day and steal her, risking his life so that they could enjoy freedom together.

Benjamin Gardner Sr. lived about two miles north of Callensburg. An ardent abolitionist, he was bold enough to conduct the fugitives in daylight. The next stop was with Elihu Chadwick of Venango County.[148] And on and on the slaves traveled until they safely reached Canada.

While the people involved in the abolitionist movement kept their actions secret, when Benjamin Gardner died in 1894 at the age of ninety-three, his obituary acknowledged his activity as "an ardent abolitionist and [a man] prominently identified with the 'underground railway' system...used in assisting fugitive slaves through this county in which were stations used for that purpose."[149]

Clearfield County, Pennsylvania

In about 1820, an immigrant from Ireland, George Atchison, settled on land in Clearfield County on the riverbank near Burnside. As a young man in Ireland, he shot some game on a gentleman's estate, which was against the law. In order to avoid prosecution, he came to America, first making his way to Centre County. Marrying in Centre County, he, along with his wife and child, moved to Clearfield County. It was his custom to travel back to Centre County for work, often leaving his family alone for weeks at a time while he earned money to buy many needed goods, which he carried home on his back. Eventually, he purchased a large tract of land and in 1845 built a home on the side of a hill near his original log cabin.[150]

Having grown up in Ireland under oppressive tenant laws, he was antislavery in this country and became one of the conductors on the Underground Railroad.[151] George Atchison was a member of the Methodist Church in his early life; however, his hatred for slavery was so great that he made the decision not to stay in a church that permitted fellowship with slave owners. As a result, he joined the Wesleyan Methodist Church, of which he remained a member the rest of his life.[152]

His house was built as two structures, with the gable of one house against the side of the other one story lower. A hall ran down one side of the upper house, near the stairs, with a space three or four feet wide taken away from the stair landing. From this space, a passage was created to a false room in

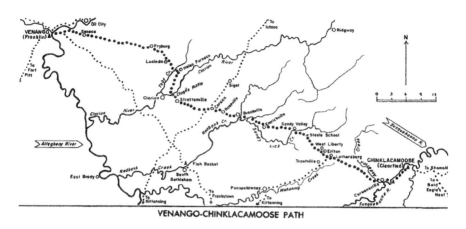

VENANGO-CHINKLACAMOOSE PATH

A map of the Venango Path as it appears in *Indian Paths of Pennsylvania* by Paul A.W. Wallace. *Pennsylvania Historic and Museum Commission, Harrisburg, Pennsylvania.*

the lower house. From the outside of the house, just above the roof of the lower house, a small window could be viewed from the river. It apparently never occurred to anyone that there was never a light shining on the inside of the window until a time after the Civil War, when the false room was discovered by new owners.[153]

Atchison would forward fugitive slaves on to the town of Clearfield. Others involved in the Underground Railroad included William Atchison, Isaac Cochran, James Gallaker, William Westover and Jason Kirk and his sons.[154]

The old Indian path from Clearfield that eventually reached Franklin was the Venango-Chinklacamoose Path.[155] Venango is a corruption of the Indian name Onenge, meaning "a mink."[156] Chinklacamoose is the Indian name for Clearfield, with some saying that the name is a corruption of Achtschingi-clamme, meaning "it almost joins," referring to the Susquehanna River, or another translation in which it means "large laughing moose."[157] This path was a branch of the Great Shamokin Path, which ran across Pennsylvania. It left the main path at the Big Spring near Luthersburg and ran to Brookville in Jefferson County.[158]

Clinton County, Pennsylvania

Clinton County has a history that spans centuries. "Various [American Indian] burial grounds have been found in this county at different points on the West Branch [of the Susquehanna River] and its tributaries. The largest of these was situated at the site of the present Lock Haven where many skeletons were unearthed when the workmen were digging the old canal. These ancient burial grounds were also found along Quinn's Run and below the mouth of Bald Eagle Creek, at McElhatten and at various points along Pine Creek."[159]

Lock Haven, the county seat, was founded in 1833. In its early years, Lock Haven was heavily involved in timber/logging industries, including rafting timber to markets downriver. Over the years, the town became famous as the home of Piper Aircraft Corporation and Lock Haven University. In 1979, Memorial Park was added to the National Register of Historic Places as an archaeological site of Native American activity.

Lock Haven is known for something more. The West Branch of the Susquehanna River was an active location for the Underground Railroad, with fugitive slaves traveling over the old Great Shamokin Path between Williamsport, Lycoming County, to a station in Lock Haven, Clinton County.

Historians have stated that because assisting runaway slaves was a crime, there isn't a lot of documented evidence of harboring the fugitives.[160] However, the life of one stationmaster, Maria Molson, was publicly documented at the time of her death. Born in Lycoming County on January 30, 1825, she was a free African American woman who eventually owned a property in Lock Haven at 19 East Water Street.[161]

A member of the Great Island Presbyterian Church, Maria died on

The Great Shamokin Path Historic Marker. *Courtesy of Wikimedia Commons.*

November 30, 1890. Her obituary provided the details of this courageous woman. "In the days before the war of the Rebellion, her house was a refuge for runaway slaves who were fleeing to Canada to escape from bondage. As many as seventeen runaway slaves have been concealed in her house at one time, and she has often related how she dressed the wounded backs of the refugees suffering from the whippings received only a few days before they made their escape from their cruel masters."[162]

Once the home of Maria Molson, 19 East Water Street, Lock Haven, Pennsylvania. *realtor.com.*

Beyond her own service, Maria's third husband, David Molson, fought in the Civil War, mustering in on September 9, 1861, with Company B, 48th Infantry. He gave his life in service to the Union on January 19, 1864.[163]

There is also evidence that Reverend Joseph Nesbitt, who was pastor of the Great Island Presbyterian Church from 1860 until 1894,[164] helped a parishioner hide slaves as well. Nesbitt's journal, held at the Ross Library in Lock Haven, appears to show that he was a man with secrets, as it is written in a shorthand that is almost impossible to read, along with the use of certain code words. In looking over his journal, it is evident he was a man of conscience—"Nesbitt also agonizes over the difference between man's law and God's law, suggesting that he was breaking the law for a greater good."[165]

Elk County, Pennsylvania

Ridgway, the county seat of Elk County, is located along the Clarion River. In 1996, 51.7 miles of the river received designation as a National Wild and Scenic River.[166] During the Civil War years, the river was important in the lumber industry. Ridgway was also the halfway mark for a stagecoach route between Warren and Clearfield.

In 1854, Nelson Gardner and his wife, Mary, made their way to Ridgway from New York State, settling on the outskirts of town in an area known locally as Montmorenci in Ridgway Township.

Nelson Gardner was a professional hunter and supplied city markets with game for many years. He is reported to have killed the last panther in Elk County between Spring Creek and Millstone Townships in 1857. The house he built was paid for with the proceeds from his profession, and it is a fine example of an early farm home. A little-known fact is that the house contained a secret room that was used to hide runaway slaves on their way to Canada.

The house was the regular stagecoach stop known as "Halfway House" along the road that is today designated as State Route 948, definitely a North Star Way.[167] Another feature of the stop was that the house was described as a "hostelry," or an inn.[168]

What was it about Nelson Gardner and his wife that caused them to become stationmasters providing a station for Underground slaves? He is remembered in the local newspapers for growing fine crops of potatoes at his home farm, serving on several juries and even once being a member of the school board. Several times, advertisements were placed for a teacher at

Nelson Gardner House, Montmorenci Road. *Dennis McGeehan, "Ridgway through Time," 2018.*

the brick school just down the road from his farm, and in the 1860 census, a schoolteacher was living at his residence.

Searching posted family trees on ancestry.com has not provided any clues, with the exception that one of Nelson's siblings was John Wesley Gardner. Does this provide a clue that perhaps he had been raised in the Methodist faith? Many Methodists of that era were abolitionists. Whatever his reasons, he should be remembered for his bold actions—by harboring slaves, he was in defiance of the federal Fugitive Slave Act, subject to fine and/or arrest.

There were three principal Underground Railroad systems in Pennsylvania from about 1840 to 1860: the Western Route, the Central Route and the Eastern Route. Elk County was on the Western Route, along with twenty-four other counties. Fugitives making their way via the Western Route were primarily from Maryland and Virginia.[169]

Charley Matthews was born into slavery in Maryland. He served as coachman to his wealthy owner, but Charley longed to be free and eventually escaped to Pittsburgh in Allegheny County, one of the twenty-five counties on the Western Route. While in Pittsburgh, he met his future wife, Mashie, and in 1854 the young couple made their way to Ridgway. Charley was hardworking and became involved in lumbering and rafting, becoming one of the most reliable pilots on the Clarion and Allegheny Rivers. The couple saved their money and bought property at the east end of Ridgway, where they built a home. Both were well liked by the citizens of Ridgway. For thirty years, they were the only Black family in town.[170] There is no evidence for why the young couple settled in Ridgway other than they stumbled across the town while heading north to Canada. There is no information about their means of arrival. Did they walk, traveling the early roads and Indian paths, come concealed on the stagecoach or perhaps follow the Allegheny and Clarion Rivers?

Free Blacks were counted in the 1850 and the 1860 census. The 1860 census provides additional clues on Charley and Mashie, shedding more light on them, as it was the first census to be conducted after their arrival in Ridgway. Charley was born in about 1825 in Maryland, and Mashie was born in about 1831 in Pennsylvania. To that end, Mashie may have been free. However, Charley was definitely a fugitive slave, unless his master had freed him sometime after his escape. What is interesting is that the census taker counted them both as white citizens. Was this an overzealous census taker who wanted to record every person in Ridgway, or someone who may have also been protecting them by identifying them as white?

An 1878 article in the *Elk County Advocate* reveals that Charley was living the life of an average citizen of Ridgway when it reported on the success of local grape growers, namely Judge Dickinson, Charley and Harry Wilson.[171]

Charley died in 1899. An endearing account about him surfaced in Brookville following his death. L.C. Scott, a local barber, reminisced about meeting Charley when he was a boy. The story was told in the local newspaper:

> *About 1865 he went with his parents to Beech Bottom on the Clarion River where they lived some time, his father engaged at lumbering. Soon after settling at Beech Bottom, Lew, who was only a boy, went with a couple of older persons to Ridgway one day, spending several hours there. Charles Matthews, the colored man referred to, was then at Ridgway, and being the only negro in the town, attracted a good deal of attention, and was talked with a great deal. Young Scott listened to Matthews talking that day, and heard him tell how he had been a slave—that he hadn't been a common field hand, but was somewhat of a favorite with his master, and as such had been permitted to carry a watch.*
>
> *Right there Scott conceived the idea that carrying a watch was a badge of distinction, and from that day forward longed to possess one.[172]*

Apparently childless, Mashie lived on in Ridgway without Charley for a number of years, disappearing from the record after 1910.

Forest County, Pennsylvania

"Forest County is home to the largest tract of the 500,000-acre Allegheny National Forest....Marienville is the gateway to the Allegheny National Forest."[173]

This broad expanse of land is lightly populated. According to the 2020 census, the population of Forest County was 6,973. The population per square mile, based on a land area of 427.6 square miles, was 16.3.[174] It is the third-smallest county by population in Pennsylvania.[175] In 1860, the year before the beginning of the Civil War, the population of Forest County was 988.[176]

Forest County was originally formed from part of Jefferson County in 1848. It was reported that wild land sold for fifty cents to two dollars per acre.[177] Pioneer Cyrus Blood first brought his family into the wilderness in 1833. His farm became known as Blood Settlement.[178] Blood was an educated man and had been a professor at Dickinson Law College in

Cyrus Blood. *From McKnight's* A Pioneer Outline History of Northwestern Pennsylvania *(1905).*

Carlisle, Pennsylvania. A farmer, he served Forest County as a surveyor, commissioner and associate judge.[179] He also became the community mail carrier, owned a tavern, taught school and operated a gristmill.[180]

When Blood purchased his tract of land from a land company, there was an understanding that a road would be opened for him. When he arrived, he found no road. Leaving his family behind in Corsica, he made his way to Clarington with an ox team, sled and men to cut their way through the wilderness twelve miles to where he would build his home. When the men reached the land Blood had purchased, the ground was cleared and a log cabin built. In October 1833, the Blood family had a new home in the wilderness.[181] This background is provided to illustrate the remoteness of the area in those early years.

One of the men who helped him cut the road through the wilderness was J.D. Hunt, who eventually married Cyrus Blood's daughter, Marien. The name of Blood Settlement was changed to Marienville in honor of her. Marienville was the first county seat of Forest County. Eventually, additional land from Venango County was added to the original Forest County, and the county seat was moved to Tionesta.[182]

The village of Clarington in Forest County is about twelve miles from Brookville in Jefferson County. It is of note as it was the home for a man named William Coon. Once fugitive slaves left Brookville, Coon and his wife would ferry the slaves over the Clarion River and feed them, providing rest and then sending them through the wilderness to Warren, Pennsylvania, for their next stop on the trip to Canada.[183]

There is also some evidence that fugitive slaves received aid in the Marienville area after they left Clarington. In a letter dated December 15, 1856, from John D. Hunt, the son-in-law of Cyrus Blood and Marienville resident, to Erastus Barnes in the town of Barnes, Hunt asks Barnes to accept a fugitive slave whom he had sheltered in Marienville. Hunt was cofounder of the Presbyterian Church in Marienville.[184]

The routes leaving Brookville heading north toward Forest County followed various Indian paths that were utilized to push the fugitives on to freedom. The Catawba Path led north to Sigel and passed very near Clarington on the way to Highland Corners in Elk County, passing near East Kane in McKean County, eventually reaching Olean.[185]

The Goschgoschink Path ran from Brookville through Corsica, passing the Clarion River at Clew's Riffle, about two miles east of Clarion. Continuing north, it eventually passed through West Hickory on its way to Warren.[186] Also known as Goshgoshing, the meaning of the word is "place of the hogs."[187]

The Venango-Chinklacamoose Path, mentioned in the section on Clearfield County, ran through Brookville to Corsica, Strattanville and on to Franklin, northward.[188]

Jefferson County, Pennsylvania

No more master's call for me,
No more, no more. No more driver's lash for me,
No more, no more. No more auction-block for me,
No more, no more. No more bloodhounds hunt for me,
No more, no more, I'm free, I'm free at last; at last,
Thank God, I'm free.[189]

Jefferson County's residents were early participants in the Underground Railroad. Indian trails that crossed the county also functioned as North Star Ways on the trek by slaves into Canada. The Venango-Chinklacamoose Path was a branch of the Great Shamokin Path running from Clearfield through Brookville to Venango (Franklin).[190]

Several people were involved in the Underground Railroad in Jefferson County years prior to the Civil War. Among them were Isaac Carmalt (a relative of William Penn) and his wife, Quakers, of Clayville, near Punxsutawney; Judge Elijah Heath and his wife, Methodists, from Brookville; Arad Pearsall and his wife, Jefferson County jailer and Methodist abolitionist; James Steadman and his wife, treasurer of Jefferson County; Reverend Christopher Fogle and his wife, Methodists, of Brookville; and James Minish of Punxsutawney.[191]

$150 REWARD
ESCAPED from the jail of Jefferson County, Pennsylvania, last night—a black man, called Charles Brown, a slave to the infant heirs of Richard

Baylor, deceased, late of Jefferson County, Virginia; he is about 5 feet 7 inches high, and 24 years of age, of a dark complexion—pleasant look, with his upper teeth a little open before. I was removing him to the State of Virginia, by virtue of a certificate from Judges Shippen, Irvin & M'Kee, of the Court of Common Pleas of the County of Venango, as my warrant to return him to the place from which he fled. I will give a reward of $150, to any person, who will deliver him to the Jailor of Jefferson County, Virginia; and if that sum should appear to be inadequate to the expense and trouble, it shall be suitably increased. John Yates, Guardian of the said heirs, September 15, 1834.[192]

This was one of two advertisements placed in the *Jeffersonian* in Brookville on September 15, 1834. The other was for a slave by the name of William Parker, alias Robinson. Both were runaway slaves who had been handed over by two slavers to the Jefferson County jailor for safekeeping. Also in the jail that September was a local resident, Butler Amos, serving time for theft.

In those years, the jail was constructed of stone, with wooden doors with iron locks. Prisoners were usually shackled and handcuffed. Judge Heath, Arad Pearsall and James Steadman somehow convinced or bribed prisoner Amos to assist them in setting the slaves free. The three provided Amos with augers and files, and Amos did the rest, filing the shackles off the slaves. Boring through the doors, Amos was able to get the locks off. The slaves were free to make their way to Canada. The slave hunters found the fugitive slaves missing in the morning.

To ensure that the slaves had a good head start, James Steadman had the two slavers who later advertised for the return of the slaves, John Yates and Stephen Delgarn, arrested for traveling on Sunday. A trial before a justice of the peace gave Parker and Brown a head start on their trek to Canada. They were successful in reaching freedom.

Someone from Brookville reported the actions of Heath, Pearsall and Steadman to the two slavers, and eventually a suit was brought into the U.S. District Court for Western Pennsylvania.[193] With the 1793 Fugitive Slave Act still law, Judge Heath, James Steadman and Arad Pearsall were found guilty. They were fined $2,000 for organizing the escape of the slaves.[194]

Judge Heath is remembered as an "outspoken abolitionist and judge" on a Pennsylvania Historic Marker, placed in front of the home he once owned at 64 Pickering Street in Brookville.

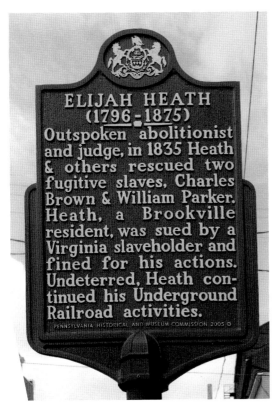

Left: Elijah Heath (1796–1875) Historic Marker, May 27, 2011. *Mike Wintermantel and www.hmdb.org*

Below: Elijah Heath House. *Wikimedia Commons.*

Lycoming County, Pennsylvania

There are people who stand as giants among men, not just because of their size but also because of their actions. One such man was named Daniel Hughes. Described as being between six feet, seven inches and six feet, ten inches tall and weighing nearly three hundred pounds,[195] he was of mixed race, including Mohawk. In the 1860 census, he was listed as a "mulatto."

Daniel Hughes was heavily involved in the Underground Railroad in Lycoming County, Pennsylvania. A man of courage, he and his wife and children took great risks to help runaway slaves.

Lycoming County, because of its location, was an important stop on the Underground Railroad. Two main areas were centers for activity: the Pennsdale-Muncy area and an area north of Williamsport where Daniel Hughes lived.

Hughes, married to Anna Rotch, a Black woman, was a lumber river raftsman on the Susquehanna River. Rafting between Williamsport and Havre de Grace, Maryland, gave him an opportunity to assist fugitive slaves. On his way back to Williamsport, the river provided him with an opportunity to direct fugitive slaves to his home, where they were hidden.

Freedom Road cemetery marker, Lycoming County, Pennsylvania. *Paul Crumlish and www. hmdb.org.*

Some were also concealed in a series of caves located near his property until they could be moved on. Hughes's son, Robert, would take the fugitives north to another station.[196]

A network of agents was at work in the Williamsport area. Abraham and Derek Updegraff towed barges on the canal that provided passage to fugitive slaves. Near an inn owned by Thomas Lightfoot, the Updegraffs would hide the slaves in a tunnel. Later, Lightfoot would move them to the Updegraff farm, where they stayed in a barn. These fugitive slaves were then taken to the home of Daniel Hughes.[197]

Others involved in the Underground Railroad in the Williamsport area were George Roach, a Black man who operated paddleboats on the canal; Charles W. Scates, a prominent lawyer; and David and Philip Roderick, who lived near Daniel Hughes.[198]

Three routes from Williamsport led to either Elmira, New York; Olean, New York; or Corning, New York.[199]

During those years before the Civil War, there were racial tensions in the Susquehanna River area. In April 1842, the Muncy Abolition Riot occurred at a schoolhouse when local tanner and abolitionist Eric Hawley invited an unknown abolitionist speaker to present a program. The presentation was interrupted when a large group of proslavery supporters began pelting the building with rocks and other projectiles, including eggs. The windows were broken, and Hawley and the speaker were injured. Fleeing the building and making their way to Hawley's home in Muncy, he and the speaker were pursued by the angry crowd lobbing eggs at them. The disturbance continued after midnight, while the two men were hiding inside Hawley's home. Eighteen were arrested, accused and indicted on charges of rioting and disturbing the peace. The trial began in September of that year. Following deliberation by the jury, an initial vote was taken, with the jurors voting eleven to one to dismiss the charges. The lone holdout was Benjamin Updegraff. Discovering that three of the jurors could barely speak English, Updegraff spoke to them in their native languages, persuading them to reconsider the evidence. After much debate and three votes, the jurors recommended conviction of thirteen of the eighteen who had been charged. The court carried out the conviction. Not long after the trial, Governor David Rittenhouse Porter pardoned the convicted defendants, stating that the abolitionist's speech was inciteful and designed to break the peace.[200]

McKean County, Pennsylvania

Ceres, located in McKean County, where the first attempt at settlement was made in 1798, became an important Underground Railroad depot.

During the abolition movement, sympathizers gathered at the King settlement above Ceres. As early as 1827 or 1828, Smethport in McKean County was a way station along the escape route to Canada.[201] A remarkable account of the bravery of the citizens of the region is recounted here:

Runaway slaves striking the Allegheny River at Warren, would take a short cut, the one used by lumbermen in this region returning from Pittsburgh, and reaching what was then known as the "Four Corners" pass through Smethport, Eldred and Olean, and so on by way of Buffalo to Canada. It was at the above mentioned that four forlorn looking slaves, foot sore and weary, and terribly hungry withal, arrived in the little village of Smethport, and stopped at a hotel kept by David Young. They acknowledged that they were runaway slaves, fleeing from hard-hearted masters, and were also out of money. Through the kindness of several of the people of Smethport, the negroes were provided with a good meal at a hotel, a small amount of money furnished them, and were sent on their way. The next stopping place was in Olean, at the hotel kept by Backus. Fearing pursuit from their masters, the slaves were directed to a lumber camp about one mile from the village, which shelter they used for a hiding place and also intended to make it their resting place for the night. Hardly had these four negroes left Smethport when two men on horseback arrived in pursuit, they being the owners of the runaways. Getting no information from the Smethport people, the horsemen hastened to Olean, at such place they arrived just as the slaves had entered their hiding place, though unseen by their masters—and here comes the gist of our tale. The citizens of Olean, who were aware of the pursuit, and fearing that the negroes might be captured, employed a little strategy for the occasion. Sending messengers to the camp with information about the state of matters, the slaves speedily sought their safety. In the meantime, the slave owners were informed that the objects of their pursuit might be found in a certain camp near Olean, and kind hands directed their course to the desired point. But upon their arrival, a sad fate awaited them. A bucket of tar and a quantity of feathers were in readiness, and masked men spread the unsightly covering without stint upon the persons of the slave owners, and then left them to their own musings. The next seen of the pursuers, who by this time had become sadder, but wiser men, was in a hotel kept by John Lee nearby where the bridge crosses the Allegheny at Eldred. Through grease, soap, water and other appliances and a sojourn of a week, the unfortunate slave owners presented a somewhat better appearance and departed for their Southern homes, and their poor slaves reached the Mecca of their hopes in Canada.[202]

One fugitive slave who traveled through McKean County for whom there is an account was Henry Rankin. In Kentucky, he was a good blacksmith. He was so good at his trade that his master allowed him to find work for himself by paying $30 per month to his master for his time while he made other earnings. His master agreed to emancipate Henry for the sum of $1,500 out of the extra proceeds of his earnings. Henry dutifully paid the $30 every month, and on each Christmas Day he gave his master all of the money he had left from the extra wages. Henry also found time after work to educate himself and became a good reader and writer.[203]

When Henry was twenty-eight years old, he had nearly paid the $1,500 for his emancipation and was looking forward to the next Christmas Day, when he would make his final payment and receive his freedom. Before that day arrived, Henry's master died. The laws of the State of Kentucky did not allow for contracts to be made with or by slaves. The heirs refused to acknowledge Henry's claim. Seizing him, they sent him to the slave market in New Orleans, where it was anticipated that he would sell for between $3,000 and $5,000 because of his value as a mechanic.

Still in bondage, Henry never gave up his hope for freedom, if need be as a fugitive slave. His opportunity came when he boarded a ship in New Orleans to make repairs. Hiding aboard, it was about five days out in the Gulf of Mexico when Henry was discovered. The captain and crew respected him for the work he did, and they dropped him in Baltimore with some advice on the best route to Canada. With some money in hand, Henry wrote his own pass to leave Baltimore and traveled into Pennsylvania. Eventually, he arrived in Bradford, McKean County. Passing the Allegheny Indian Reservation, he arrived in Springville, New York, eventually making his way to Canada. Henry made his escape at the time the Underground Railroad was first organized and found his way without its assistance.[204]

Potter County, Pennsylvania

Potter County is known locally as "God's country" and boasts what is known as the Highway to the Stars, an area passing through Cherry Creek State Park where it is said the Milky Way shines so bright thousands of stars can be seen in the night skies.[205] It was also on the route of the Underground Railroad, part of the central route, with slaves coming primarily from Maryland and Virginia via the Susquehanna River in Harrisburg:[206]

> *Coudersport…was an important point on the Underground.…It has always been hard to get particulars as to persons engaged in this work.… They had been engaged in an unlawful business, violating the laws of…the United States. Aside from this they were of the best law-abiding citizens. Their views of liberty and the rights of man compelled them to do one thing which the law condemned, but their hearts approved, and they were very sensitive about the matter.*[207]

John S. Mann was an attorney, Quaker and stationmaster in the Underground Railroad, as well as the owner of a two-story property at the southwest corner of Third and Main Street in Coudersport built a few years before the 1850 Fugitive Slave Act was passed. The house had a secret room accessible from the roof of the single-story part of the house where slaves entered through a loose board in the wall.[208] Slaves leaving Coudersport then headed to Ceres in McKean County for another safe stop along the way.

John Mann's brother, Joseph Mann, who operated a large store in Millport, about twelve miles from Coudersport, was also involved in hiding slaves for short periods of time, and John Mann's wife was always ready to assist. One of their children in later years remarked that it was not unusual to find a fugitive slave at the breakfast table.

In one instance, a female fugitive slave was brought to Coudersport by an abolitionist. The woman had been with several other members of her family, but near Williamsport, the pursuit of them was so close that the family members were forced to separate. The woman remained a week at the Mann House, assisting with housework and resting up from the long trip.

To leave Coudersport, the fugitive was dressed in some of Mrs. Mann's clothes. A sympathetic female neighbor took the Mann horse and buggy and drove the woman more than one hundred miles to Buffalo, staying with friends along the way. She turned the fugitive over to an abolitionist,

John S. Mann's home. *Schmidt Family Tree, originally shared by Lyle Beefelt, November 19, 2008, Ancestry.com.*

who got her across the border to Canada.

The Mann home earned a reputation as a place for escaped slaves. One evening, a man stopped by the residence, noting that he was an officer looking for an escaped slave and that he was going to search the house. Mann agreed but asked to see his search warrant. The man replied that he didn't need a search warrant as he was a government official and made some threats against Mann, who held his ground saying that the officer could not search without the proper search warrant. The official left and never returned.

One evening before the outbreak of war, a runaway slave entered John Mann's law office, dropping into a chair. It was evident to Mann that the man had nearly lost hope. His boots were worn out, with the soles and upper part being held together with strings around his feet. His clothes barely covered his body. He told Mann that for a week he had been dodging his master and a U.S. marshal. Managing to say ahead of them, he slept in the woods, not finding any shelter where residents would take him in for fear of the law.[209]

Knowing that the man desperately needed help, John Mann also knew that if the slavers were close by, his home would be one of the first places they would search. Mann had a male employee, Pat, working for him. Pat was an Irishman and a Democrat. He didn't express a lot of empathy for fugitive slaves. Mann thought about the situation and asked Pat to take the fugitive to his house, but he refused. Pat also said that his wife would refuse to have the fugitive in their home. The two bantered back and forth for a time, Mann describing what would happen to the slave if he was captured. Still unmoved, John eventually reminded Pat that it was Mrs. Mann, John's wife, who helped Pat's family when his child was ill. That convinced Pat to take the fugitive to his house, apparently convincing his wife to do this favor for Mr. Mann after his wife had helped them earlier. The fugitive was there longer than usual over concerns that the slavers might return. Pat reported to Mann every day on the fugitive's condition. When it was considered safe to travel, the man made his way to Canada, with the news of his arrival coming back weeks later.[210]

Tioga County, Pennsylvania

Tioga County was formed from parts of Lycoming County on March 26, 1804.[211] The name Tioga is a corruption of the Native American word De-yoh-ho-gah, meaning "where it forks or at the forks," used in reference to the river, county, township and town and also the name of a former Indian village in Bradford County.[212]

Wellsboro, the county seat, is just twelve miles east of the Pennsylvania Grand Canyon. The county boasts seven lakes and thousands of acres of state forest.

Wellsboro was founded by Benjamin Wistar Morris, who was born in Philadelphia. He was a member of the Society of Friends, otherwise known as Quakers. Having met with financial reversals in Philadelphia, he decided to settle on land he owned in Tioga Township, Lycoming County, which is now Tioga County. In 1799, Morris, along with his wife, Mary Wells Morris, and two children, Rebecca and Samuel, succeeded in establishing a new home in the wilderness. The town was named Wellsboro in honor of his wife.[213]

Although Morris's son, Samuel Wells Morris, was about thirteen years of age when he arrived in the region, he received an education at Princeton College. Samuel was described as a man of "great activity and enterprise." He was the first treasurer of the county and its first postmaster, was elected a county commissioner, served as judge and was member of the Pennsylvania legislature.[214]

While there is some history of a few slaves having been brought into Tioga County by early settlers, they were manumitted—that is, had been given their freedom.[215]

In 1828–29, two young Black men arrived in Wellsboro along with two Black boys, all fugitive slaves. The latter two moved on, finding employment near Covington. The first two were put to work by Judge Morris and remained a month or more with the judge.[216]

Samuel W. Morris. *From Brown's History of Tioga County, Pennsylvania (1897).*

Two unidentified escaped slaves wearing ragged clothes, 1861. *Library of Congress.*

The townspeople were shocked when they learned that men from Maryland had arrived in the village claiming to be the owners of the slaves and armed with writs for their arrest signed by Judge Kilburn of Lawrenceville. Word went out to the fugitives, and they fled the town, headed for Covington, but were stopped by two deputy sheriffs. Brought back to the village, the two were handcuffed and fitted with irons brought by their owners. The party started off to see Judge Kilburn but were followed by Judge Morris to "see fair play." The citizens of Wellsboro discussed the situation, offering suggestions for action on behalf of the fugitives. Some wanted to have the hearing in Wellsboro and suggested filing a writ of habeas corpus returnable before Judge Morris. A clerk in the Prothonotary's Office drew up the writ and gave it to men who were going to take it to Judge Morris at Lawrenceville. When the men arrived at the tavern in Lawrenceville, they learned that the slave owners were upstairs in the tavern.[217]

The capture of slaves in Tioga County hadn't happened before. People believed that when runaways made it to northern states, they would be free. Many of the people thought the fugitives should receive fair treatment, that their shackles should be taken off and the sheriff should be an umpire, allowing a fair fight for the slaves against their masters. But the sheriff would not agree. Harsh words were exchanged and threats made, and with all of the shouting, the slave owners appeared downstairs with their pistols drawn. The sheriff informed the slave owners that he knew the people of Tioga County better than they did and to put their pistols away or he would put them under arrest to save their lives, noting that if one shot were fired, he could not be answerable for their safety. He advised that if they valued their lives more than their slaves, they had better leave the defense of their property in his hands, saying, "You will be dead men in less than ten minutes after the first shot is fired!" Apparently, the men from Maryland took him seriously and moved back into a corner. Suddenly, someone in the crowd extinguished the lights, and the fugitive slaves were hurried out the door away from their captors and over the New York state line.[218]

The next morning, a warrant was issued for the arrest of the men involved in aiding the fugitives. A court case followed, as the slave owners claimed that they were deprived of their property. A paper was drawn up and signed that stipulated that upon payment of twenty-five dollars by one of the defendants, it would be considered full satisfaction in the matter. The men from Maryland saw that they were defeated and departed.

The two rescued slaves fled to a point near Rochester and obtained employment at a tavern. The slave owners, however, instead of heading south as they had indicated, headed north, still intent on finding the fugitives. Judge Morris, suspecting that the slave owners had learned of the location of the fugitives, interceded and took passage on the stage with the slave owners heading toward Rochester. After a time, Judge Morris claimed to be ill and asked the stage to stop at a place that was a few miles from the tavern where the slaves were working. Taking a private room, Judge Morris asked the landlord to detain the stage under the pretense that he would soon be well enough to go on. Feigning a more serious illness, however, Judge Morris used the time to hitch up a team to make his way to the tavern, where he advised the fugitives that their masters were in pursuit. It gave them time to move beyond their reach. When the delayed stage eventually arrived at the tavern, Judge Morris, who was standing on the porch, politely bowed to the slave owners. As they stepped off the stage, they realized that they had been outwitted by the judge.[219]

In addition to this activity in the early years of its history, Tioga County was on the Williamsport to Corning route of the Underground Railroad. Daniel Hughes and his son, Robert, directed the fugitives from their home in Williamsport along Lycoming Creek north to Trout Run. From there, the trail continued through Grover and Canton in Bradford County. The fugitives walked the whole distance or were transported in false-bottom carriages. Arriving in Tioga County, the Putnam family in the northern part of the county sheltered fugitives in a secret room reached by a winding staircase. William Garretson of the town of Tioga, a lawyer and member of the Pennsylvania legislature, was a stationmaster and conductor. Nearby in Delmar Township, Israel and Amanda Stone kept a station in their home.[220]

Warren County, Pennsylvania

During the third week in June, a small village outside of Warren, Pennsylvania, celebrates a two-day festival, the Sugar Grove Underground Railroad Convention. It commemorates the Sugar Grove Anti-Slavery Convention of June 1854, which Frederick Douglass, the famed abolitionist who was in attendance, called "the crowning convention of them all."[221]

Frederick Douglass was the son of a slave, Harriet Bailey. He was a self-educated man, and his poor treatment infused him with a hatred for slavery. In 1836, he attempted to escape but failed. Two years later, he was successful and reached New Bedford, Massachusetts, where he changed his surname to Douglass. Known for his oratory skills, he became involved in the Underground Railroad movement. His opponents refused to believe that he had been a slave because of his intellect and believed he was an imposter working for the abolitionists.[222]

Antislavery conventions were popular from 1830 until the time of the Civil War. Sugar Grove was a place where many abolitionists lived, and it became a safe haven for slaves making their way to Canada. More than five hundred people attended the outdoor Sugar Grove Convention. While there, Frederick Douglass had tea in the home of Cynthia Catlin Miller, an active member of the Sugar Grove Aid Society, a group that sewed clothes for escaping slaves.[223]

On June 23, 1854, Douglass published an account of his time at Sugar Grove:

> *The crowning Convention was held Saturday and Sunday, in a beautiful grove in Sugar Grove, Warren County, Pennsylvania, about three miles from Busti. The responsibility of getting up this meeting rested upon the Storom family at Busti—an enterprising family of farmers, well to do on the world and when I tell you that these industrious and well to do farmers are of the color of you and me, you will…draw from it the right hopes for our whole people.*
>
> *I observed that this family (it is a large one) had so deported itself, that white people among whom they moved, appeared to regard and treat them precisely as respectable people ought to be treated….*
>
> *But a word of the Convention; it was, as I have said, the crowning one of all….The meeting was strictly a religious Anti-Slavery meeting, and left a most favorable impression for the cause.*[224]

Tom Stowe was a fugitive slave who traveled through Warren, Pennsylvania, to reach freedom in Canada. Tom's master, a plantation owner in Vicksburg, Mississippi, was known as a "sporting man." He was known from New Orleans to Baltimore for his racehorses, fighting dogs and fighting cocks. Tom was his top man, handling all of his stock. He was such a valuable slave that his master refused to sell him, even though he was offered $3,000 for him.

The trips with his master took Tom to many locations over the years. When Tom had the occasion to visit Morgantown, West Virginia, the grocer he bought supplies from talked to him about a passage to Canada and freedom, apparently having a connection with the Underground Railroad. Tom, ever loyal to his master, determined that his master couldn't spare him.[225]

Left: Cynthia Catlin Miller. *Find A Grave, added by C.A. Brown.*

Right: Frederick Douglass before 1855. *Wikimedia Commons.*

Tom had a wife, Lucy, and a son, Georgie. His wife had been raised in the household and was a maid to the master's wife. The master allowed the marriage between Lucy and Tom in the hopes of keeping Tom from the Underground Railroad, whose depots they often passed on their trips along the Ohio River. It was while Tom was away on business to bring back colts that had been purchased by the master that the master sold Tom's three-year-old son to a slave trader, apparently in a fit of rage because Lucy would not be unfaithful to Tom. When Tom returned to the plantation, he not only found his son gone but also his wife ill, and she soon died from a broken heart. With his happiness gone, Tom buried his wife and determined to stay with his master until he could learn who had purchased his little boy. It took two years for Tom to find the slave trader, a man named Austin, who recounted that he sold Georgie at auction to a lawyer in Savannah.

Tracking him down, Tom found Georgie in the hands of a kind gentleman and lady, who was teaching him to read. They told Tom that they did not regard Georgie as a slave and that if Tom found himself in a condition to take his son with him, they would give Georgie over to him.[226] Tom's master never knew that Tom located his son.

After a period of time, Tom and his master found themselves again in Morgantown, West Virginia. While his master was keeping a close eye on him, Tom was again advised by an old friend, the grocer, not to let go of the chance to cross to the west side of the Monongahela River and make his way along the top of a mountain to Pittsburgh. His friend described how he could then access the Allegheny River, which would take him on a northern route to Canada. Tom later said that his friend didn't tell him that the Allegheny River didn't reach all the way to Canada.

Tom took off in his quest for freedom in the North, avoiding contact with others, particularly white people. On the third day, six men stumbled upon him, and realizing that he was a runaway fugitive slave worth $2,000, they ordered him to surrender. Tom fought back fiercely and escaped. He continued his journey, following the Allegheny River, until he was near Franklin. There he saw another Black man coming toward him. While he was very wary, Tom was half starved and asked if the man could find some bread for him. Though fearing for his life, the Black man persuaded Tom to go with him, taking him to an Underground Railroad depot nearby. Even with a sprained ankle, Tom could not be persuaded to stay until his foot recovered. He pushed through on his quest for freedom, continuing north to Franklin, through Warren and then into New York State. All along the way, he was received by conductors.[227] It is not known whether Tom ever recovered his son, Georgie, although it was suggested that if he had joined Sherman's March to the Sea across Georgia, he might have found Georgie in Savannah and been reunited.[228]

Part IV

IMPACT OF THE WAR
ON FAMILIES IN THE WILDS

LETTERS FROM SOLDIERS

Edwin Little, Jefferson County, Pennsylvania

Going home, going home,
I'm just going home
Quiet light, some still day
I'm just going home.

It's not far, just close by
Through an open door
Work all done, care laid by
Going to fear no more.

Mother's there expecting me
Father's waiting, too
Lots of folk gathered there
All the friends I knew

All the friends I knew.[229]

It appears that the initial bravado and rush to join a fighting unit was over the fact that the South seceded from the Union, not over the issue of

Home on furlough. *Smithsonian Institute, National Museum of American History, by John Sartain.*

slavery. In other words, those who stepped up and volunteered were doing so to preserve the Union, and they believed that the war would be over in a few months.

Some insight is given into the attitude of those who quickly volunteered through the letters that they sent home. One poignant series of letters is held by the Union League of Philadelphia, with a typed copy provided to the Punxsutawney Area Historical Society. The letters are from Edwin Little of Punxsutawney to his wife, Maggie. Jeffrey Lundy, a Punxsutawney attorney, collected those letters, and along with providing a narration about the events of the day (e.g., battles, downtime and so on) experienced by Edwin Little and the members of Company I, 62nd Volunteers, which influenced the letters to his wife, it provides a vivid picture of the experiences of the soldiers. In Lundy's book, *My Own Dearest Maggie: The Story of Civil War Captain Edwin Little and His Wife Maggie Told through His Letters Home,*[230] one reads about the early excitement of going off to war, how the soldiers longed for their home life and, finally, despair as the war drew on for years.

After months of battle, Edwin returned home for a ten-day furlough on January 27, 1863. Expressing his joy in a letter upon return to duty on February 17, 1863,[231] he said:

It does me so much good to set and think what a happy, pleasant time I had at home. They were the ten days of the happiest days of my life. Oh, I shall never forget them, no never. Oh, but I would love to be with you always. Always near your side. Then only am I happy, but I wish this was Over. Then all would be well. May God protect us all and soon Hasten the day when war will be at an End.[232]

He was memorialized in a history written fifteen years after his death:

He gave his life for the Union is the simple story of a brave soldier whose memory is green in the hearts of his kindred and fellow citizens. He left a wife and three children—two girls and one son—to mourn the loss of a kind husband and an indulgent father.[233]

RESIDENCE OF MRS. M. LITTLE,   D. PUNXSUTAWNEY. JEFFERSON CO. PA.

Maggie Little House, Punxsutawney, Pennsylvania. *From* Caldwell's Atlas of Jefferson County, Pennsylvania *(1878)*.

Simple words to sum up the life of one held in high esteem in his hometown of Punxsutawney. Born in 1833, he was just two months from celebrating his thirtieth birthday when his life was taken in the Battle of Gettysburg. A simple announcement appeared in the *Brookville Republican*:

> *Casualties—Up to this* [Thursday] *morning we have no report of the casualties in any of our companies, except Capt. Little, Co. I, 62d P.V., who is reported killed. Col. Dick Coulter, 11th P.V., and Col. Taylor, of the Bucktails are killed.*[234]
>
> *Punxsutawney, Pennsylvania. November 9, 1863, Edwin Thaddeus Little. Nine months after Edwin's February furlough home with his Dearest Wife Maggie, Maggie gave birth to a baby boy. She named him Edwin Thaddeus Little.*[235]

In other parts of the county, while the Little family was mourning the loss of their loved one, the *Brookville Republican* reported on the Copperheads: "We understand that the Copperheads raised a hickory pole at Haggerty's tavern, in Eldred township, on the Fourth, at which speeches denunciatory of the War and the Government were made by some able (!) speakers from this place. It surprised us to learn that the 'Stars and Stripes' were placed upon the pole, when it would certainly have been more in accordance with the whole proceedings and the teachings of the Speakers, to have run up the Stars & Bars, instead of thus desecrating the glorious Flag of the Free."[236]

George Washington Gathers, Clarion County, Pennsylvania

Lonely, I'm Mr. Lonely
I have nobody for my own
I am so lonely
I'm Mr. Lonely…

Now, I am a soldier
A lonely soldier
Away from home
Through no wish of my own
That's why I'm lonely
I'm Mr. Lonely
I wish that I could go back home

Letters, never a letter
I get no letters in the mail
I've been forgotten,
Yeah, forgotten,
Oh, how I wonder how is it I failed...[237]

George Washington Gathers was born in Clarion County in 1817.[238] He was married to Polly Mary Kifer in 1836. Over the years, they were the parents of eleven children.

Washington, as he was known, was forty-four years old when the Civil War broke out. Apparently a volunteer, he served with Company A, 103rd Regiment of Pennsylvania, enlisting in 1861 and mustering out in 1865 with the rank of sergeant.[239] In the 1860 census, the last one taken before the outbreak of war, Washington was listed as a farmer and father of seven children.

In two letters from April 1862 through May 1863, acquired at an estate sale in the fall of 2018, correspondence by Washington was written to Henry Over. Henry Over saved the letters and passed them to his son, James. Eventually, the letters ended up in the hands of Orpha Over. Orpha, born in 1910, was an elementary school teacher who in 1939 married Willis Harmon Elliott. Orpha died childless in October 1996. The letters apparently were valued through a line of succession in the Over family.

The first letter, dated April 16, 1862, from Camp Cory near Fort Monroe, describes Washington's trip from Kittanning to the Virginia Peninsula. Like many who enlisted, he expressed his belief that he would be home by July. Both letters have been transcribed as written; however, spelling has been corrected and punctuation added where necessary. The grammar remains unchanged:

I tell you that we are in the enemy country now, the rebels is only two miles from us now. We have to keep our eyes skinned here now. We are two miles from the James River and the rebels is just across the river from us....We are in camp here, yet we are under marching orders. Now we don't know how soon we will leave this, we was within 18 miles of a fight yesterday. [A] black regiment was in the fight there...we could hear them from where we are....The news came in to our camp that our men took fifteen hundred prisoners and the word came also we will come home about July if they keep on as they have.

"The Soldier's Dream of Home." *Smithsonian Institute, National Museum of America History, by Max Rosenthal and L.N. Rosenthal, publisher William Smith, Philadelphia, credit Harry T. Peters "America on Stone" Lithography Collection, 1864.*

Gathers noted that he toured the Capitol, received a smallpox vaccine and sent home sixty dollars to his wife. Writing about his daily activities and that he had been out on picket for twenty-four hours, he noted how tired he was. He closed by saying that he had to go to church.

In a letter most likely written in May 1863, he took a different tone, having participated in a number of battles and skirmishes and with his service having been extended long past July 4, 1861:

> *Come but if God spares me I hope to see the day that I can come and see you once more. I still live in that kind of hope but there are plenty more in the same kind of a fix that I am. I have had no letter from home for a long time. I don't know what is wrong. I think they must be miscarried. The last letter that I got they was all well. I suppose that I will get one before long. I am always glad to hear from some of you at home. It is a good deal of satisfaction to me to hear that you are all well. I have written John and Will several letters and they never answered them and I will not write any more till they write to me. It is not the cost of the thing. They are lazy to*

write that is all the trouble with them. I suppose the draft will make some of the boys feel a little sick by this time. I suppose that they will hate to leave their little girls. Well boys, there is a little danger here. The Rebs throw their bullets very careless. They would leave hit a fellow as not. That is so my boys. You will not have your mothers to wait on you here. Give my love to Grandpap Over. Nothing at present but remaining your friend till death.

WHEN JOHNNY COMES MARCHING HOME AGAIN: AN EARLIER GENERATION OF BABY BOOMERS?

When Johnny comes marching home again,
Hurrah! Hurrah!
We'll give him a hearty welcome then
Hurrah! Hurrah!
The men will cheer and the boys will shout
The ladies they will all turn out
And we'll all feel gay when Johnny comes marching home[240]

The front page of the *Brookville Republican* of October 19, 1864, carried various war accounts, along with a list of the most recent draftees from Jefferson County by township.

Discussion in the paper centered on the upcoming election between Abraham Lincoln and George B. McClellan, the former commander of the Union Army of the Potomac. McClellan and Lincoln had a strained relationship throughout the time McClellan served as chief of the army, resulting in many quarrels between the two men. When McClellan failed to follow Lee into Virginia after the Battle of Antietam, Maryland, in 1862, Lincoln replaced him. The Democrats nominated McClellan as their candidate for president. One article appearing in the paper that day was written from a Republican perspective and titled, "Elect Little Mac and Then—Aye! And Then Look Out for the Opening of the Sixth Seal,"[241] listing all the negatives about the Democratic candidate, including the fact that the Copperheads were in favor of his nomination and pushing for his win.

The election of 1864, to put it in context, came after the Battle of Gettysburg, which was fought July 1–3, 1863, and was notable for the fact that there was good reason to postpone the election in the midst of war. It was also the first election by absentee ballot as so many men were at the front. As reported in the paper, "The vote of fifteen hundred soldiers at Fort Snelling, Minnesota, had been taken and the votes forwarded in sealed envelopes…the vote stands—for Lincoln, one thousand two hundred, McClellan, three hundred."[242]

The list of soldiers drafted from Beaver Township included one Henry Myers. The surnames of other draftees reflect the ethnic makeup of the township at that time: Reitz, Osman, Blyler, Himes, Guthrie, Shaffer, Hetrick, Thomas, Gearhart, Smathers, Shick, Wagoner, Baughman, Sowers, Reed, Broscious, Hetrick, Motter, Lang, Cobel, Funk and Shrauger.

Born in Centre County, Pennsylvania, on September 9, 1826, to George and Mary Showalter Myers, Henry Myers was the great-grandson of Nicholas Myers, who immigrated to America from Baden-Baden, Germany, in 1737, settling in Adams County, Pennsylvania. He married Anna Margaretha Albert, who immigrated from Eckersweiler, Germany, and the family prospered, eventually owning 145 acres of land. As the family branched out, Henry's father, George, settled in Clarion County, Pennsylvania.[243]

The 1850 census recorded a twenty-three-year-old wagonmaker, Henry Myers, along with his wife, "Terry," and four-month-old daughter, Charlotte, living next door to his father in Redbank Township, Clarion County. By 1860, thirty-two-year-old Henry Myers, a wheelwright; his wife, Christena; and children John, nine; Elizabeth, three; and Matilda, ten months old, were residing in Beaver Township, Jefferson County, a thriving community of people of mostly German stock. Henry and Christena (Heist) Myers were members of the Bethlehem Evangelical Lutheran Congregation

Henry Myers, Civil War soldier. *John Myers.*

in nearby Ohl, where services were conducted in German until 1875. Church records reveal Christena's attendance and baptism of one of their daughters, and Henry Myers apparently pledged financial support for a sister church at Shannondale in Clarion County.[244]

By the time war broke out, Henry had fathered six children, four of whom were living. Family tradition records that he bought his way out of the draft on at least one occasion. As fighting intensified, Henry was drafted from July 1, 1863, until August 17, 1863. Nine months after his return home, Henry and Christena became parents again when Sara Ann was born in May 1864.

Again called in the draft, thirty-eight-year-old Henry began service on October 6, 1864, mustering out on June 29, 1865, serving with the 57th Pennsylvania Regiment, Company K. This period took him to the front near Petersburg, Virginia, where the regiment was constantly engaged in driving back the enemy, establishing new lines and erecting fortifications. Henry was near Appomattox when Lee surrendered.[245]

Another soldier from Jefferson County, Peter R. Reitz, Henry's neighbor, was also called in the draft of October 6, 1864. Peter and Henry were tent mates throughout their time of service.[246]

Peter was also of German stock, born in Jefferson County on August 6, 1835, to Johannes and Magdalene Reitz. On October 1, 1857, he married Catherine Brosious. The Reitz marriage produced four children prior to the time he was drafted.[247]

Did the soldiers return to the shouts and cheers of the citizens who remained on the homefront? The *Brookville Republican* called for celebrations to be held on the Fourth of July 1865 "to honor our brave soldiers....None deserve more credit and honor than the brave, patriotic men, who have for the last four years have absented themselves from their homes and risked their lives in defence of the Union."[248]

In Tioga County, the newspaper on June 25, 1865, announced, "Grand Celebration of the 4th of July," noting that "on the 4th of July next, at which time and place all returned soldiers of the war for national life are cordially invited to appear in uniform if possible....There will be the finest display of Martial Music ever afforded in this county and a Grand Display of Fireworks in the evening."[249]

Henry Myers was less than whole when he returned from the war. He suffered from severe rheumatism brought on by a fall into a cold creek. He was almost totally deaf in one ear, with slight deafness in the other, having been "shocked" when he didn't hear the order from his commanding officer to "Stand on your toes," which was the order when a cannon was about to be fired.[250] Henry went back to his former trade as a wheelwright, but by 1880, at the age of fifty-three, he had become a farmer.[251]

Reitz, who testified as to Henry's maladies from the war on behalf of Henry's application for an invalid pension, also suffered from disabilities. Originally a carpenter by trade, because of his severe rheumatism and as a result of the war, he turned to farming for a living.[252] In his obituary of May 1, 1900, submitted to the newspaper by a friend, Peter Reitz died three months before his sixty-fourth birthday. His wife recalled being awakened by his heavy breathing during a second attack of paralysis. The

Left: Henry Myers. *John Myers.*

Middle: Christena Heist Myers. *John Myers.*

Right: Peter Reitz. *Joanne Reitz Family Tree, photo originally shared by philip4_9, March 8, 2011, Ancestry.com.*

obituary noted that friends thought that his time in the Civil War had an effect in shortening his life.[253]

Ironically, Henry Myers died on May 22, 1900, twenty-one days after his Civil War mate and neighbor and four months before his seventy-fourth birthday. Both soldiers are buried at the Bethlehem Lutheran Church Cemetery at Ohl, Beaver Township, Jefferson County.

Researching Henry Myers's involvement in the Civil War raised a question: Did the aftermath of the Civil War produce an earlier generation of baby boomers, as did World War II? After his return to Jefferson County, Henry and Christena Myers had three additional children, for a total of eight living children, truly a "baby boom." Peter Reitz and his wife, Catherine, became the parents of eight additional children in the years following the Civil War.[254]

While other families also experienced a kind of "baby boom" after the return of soldiers, a demographer noted that there was a big change in fertility rates during the nineteenth century, when women went from having seven children in the early 1800s to having three and a half children through the end of the nineteenth century.[255]

THE HOMEFRONT

Historians estimate that half of all soldiers in the U.S. Army were farmers or farm laborers and an estimated thirty percent of all soldiers were married.[256]

There is no written record of how Christena Myers and her brood managed during the war. One might surmise that her son John, who was about thirteen in 1864, assisted his mother by taking on tasks that would have been handled by his father. It was not unusual for older children to be hired out to others needing assistance. The women would rely on receiving credit at a local store, with the bill to be paid when the soldier's pay reached his family. Neighboring women such as Peter Reitz's wife may have worked with Christena and other women to sustain their families while their men were at war. Taking in laundry or sewing and, in some instances, having boarders could help make ends meet.

Women were often in difficult situations. Soldiers' pay wasn't always forthcoming, so receiving credit from the local grocer could be challenging.

Unidentified young women in dresses in front of American flag. *Library of Congress.*

Local relief was available at the county level but could be prejudiced—the local relief boards often comprised middle-class people who were not always compassionate; wives of enlisted soldiers received different treatment than the wives of drafted men; deserters' wives were taken off the rolls, in some instances forcing the wife and her children into the county poorhouse; and women could be denied aid for lack of respectability.[257]

Esther Campman, a resident of Clearfield County, described her desperate situation in a letter to Pennsylvania governor Andrew Curtin. Writing in late April 1865, as the war was ending and with her husband gone for eight months, she was seeking the governor's assistance. "I have not received a sent yet to ceep mi family on and he never has had eney pay yet. I have worked night and Day and ceep mi children together and I have touck sick and am on able to Do enething. I truly hope you will Do something for me."[258] Campman had applied to the county for relief money. "I went to the commisherns and the[y] said the[y] woud not give me eney."[259] One can only speculate as to why she was turned down by the county. The application came late in the war and from the wife of a drafted soldier, so it was denied. Esther's husband had earlier sent a letter that he was in a military hospital in Virginia. Continuing with her correspondence to Curtin, "I have begun to think he is cilled but I dount [k]now."[260]

As the war raged on, other women in rural Pennsylvania contacted the governor's office. As one woman who was struggling to keep together a seventy-five-acre family farm explained, "I have no one to get a stick of wood or to feed or to take a bushel of grain to mill for me…and I hant able to doe any thing out in the wet with out getting pretty sick. It is actually necessary that I could get a furlough for him for 30 or 40 days to come home and help me to get a lot of wood."[261] This same woman, writing to her husband, noted that she had planted corn, oats, wheat and many other crops. "I hope dat god is with youse and kepe yous alife dat you can [re]torn onst home."[262]

There were many pleas sent to local relief boards, but oftentimes the relief was only a few dollars. One mother writing to Governor Curtin seeking additional relief said, "My little Children is naked and I am very near naked."[263]

Women on the homefront pitched in to do what they could in a variety of ways. Within the Wilds, they took part in various societies with the sole purpose of sending aid to the troops on the battlefront. In Brookville, one such organization was titled the Ladies of the Brookville Soldiers Aid Society. The local newspaper reported its support of the troops, while the ladies also "resolved at their last meeting that hereafter no political opinions or differences shall be expressed at their meetings, as they meet only for benevolent purposes, and hope all may feel interested and request this published in the Republican and Jeffersonian."[264] The Brookville aid society also called on the women in the townships to join in this work.

The Ladies Aid Society of Potter County, on September 11, 1863, sent boxes of items to the U.S. Sanitary Commission in Philadelphia. The *Potter Journal* and *News of Coudersport* reported the list of articles, which included double gowns, wrappers, flannel shirts, muslin shirts, towels, sheets, bandages and slippers, among other items, plus various food items.[265]

In Bellefonte, Centre County, the Ladies Knitting Association resolved to knit socks for the soldiers. A news article about the project requested one pair of socks or more; the socks were to be at least one-fourth pound in weight, with no white socks, and they were to be ready for shipment by the first week in November.[266]

With few written local accounts of wartime experiences, one obituary of a couple from Reynoldsville, Jefferson County, was revealing. Mrs. John Smith put her four children in an ox cart and drove from Reynoldsville to Georgia and Tennessee to be near her husband and to take care for him should he be wounded.[267]

The war changed the women left on the homefront. Forced to become more independent, going forward in the years following their husbands'

Departure from the old homestead. *Library of Congress.*

return, women became more engaged in society by taking part in political and social debates, with some even turning wartime experiences such as nursing and teaching into careers.[268]

Some families never recovered from the stresses put on them by the war. In August 1866, Frederick Campman, who had been drafted at the age of thirty-three, filed for divorce from his wife, Esther, the same woman who only a year earlier had pleaded with Governor Curtin for assistance.[269] Which one of them was so changed after their wartime experiences? Maybe both. Esther, the mother of four children, died in 1871.

SOLDIERS' ORPHAN SCHOOLS

The name "soldiers' orphan school" conjures up a mind full of visions of frail children, malnourished, poorly clothed, with no one to love them—destitute, alone in the world. An orphan is defined as "a child deprived by death of one or both parents."[270]

In Pennsylvania, following the Civil War, the state established an extensive system of orphan schools and homes to care for and educate the children of fallen soldiers, not children destitute and without both parents.

James L. Paul, the chief clerk of the Department of Soldiers' Orphan Schools and author of *Pennsylvania's Soldiers' Orphan Schools*,[271] laid out his vision for the schools: "to educate coming generations to the belief that if men fall on the battlefield or in the discharge of the duties which they owe the nation, in the defense of liberty, justice and right, a loving and God-fearing people will take their offspring to themselves as their own, and, so far as can be, fit them physically, mentally, and morally for the stern realities of this world and the enjoyments of that which lies beyond."[272] In March 1876, J.P. Wickersham, superintendent of public instruction in Harrisburg, lauded Paul's narrative telling "how a great state has expended over five millions of dollars in maintaining and educating over eight thousand children, made fatherless by the casualties of war is a laudable and grateful undertaking."[273]

There were guidelines for the admission of students, set out under an act in 1864:

Children of either sex under the age of fifteen, resident in Pennsylvania at the time of the application and dependent upon either public or private charity for support, or on the exertions of a mother or other person destitute of means to afford proper education and maintenance, of fathers who have been killed, or died of wounds received or of disease contracted in the service of the Unites States, whether in volunteer or militia regiments of this State, or in the regular army or the naval service of the United States, but who were at the time of entering such service actual bona fide residents of Pennsylvania.[274]

Guidelines outlined the kind of education and maintenance that would be afforded the children: "The Orphans will be clad in a neat, plain uniform dress, according to sex and supplied with comfortable lodgings, a sufficiency of wholesome food and proper attendance when sick; they will be physically developed—the boys by military drill or gymnastic training, according to age, and the girls by calisthenic and other suitable exercises."[275] Eventually, the original plan to include children under the age of six to be sent to primary schools was reconsidered as well, concluding that children between the ages of six and ten should attend institutions for younger children. The younger children who were destitute found refuge at organizations such as Northern Home for Friendless Children of Philadelphia, which had been helping children during the war; Children's Home in Lancaster; and Soldiers' Orphan Home in Pittsburgh, among others.[276]

In the application for admission, the mother or guardian of the child signed a document stating, "I do hereby resign and transfer to said Superintendent, and to his successors in office, the custody, care, and control of said Orphan, for said purpose till [his/her] arrival at the full age of sixteen years, with the full right to put or bind out on her [him/her] arrival at said age, for such employment or trade to such employer or master, and during such term, as said Superintendent shall then select, with the written assent of said Orphan and of myself."[277]

In Mansfield, Tioga County, Professor F.A. Allen was principal of the Mansfield Normal School. Normal schools in those years were institutions created to train teachers. What began as Mansfield Classical Seminary in 1857 had by 1862 become the Mansfield Normal School, the third such state school in Pennsylvania. Moving through time, in 1927, the name Mansfield Normal School was officially changed to Mansfield State Teachers College, today known as Mansfield University of Pennsylvania.[278]

Learning that the state had made provisions for the establishment of solders' orphan schools, Professor Allen applied for twenty-five boys and twenty-five girls. Granted permission by the state to open an orphan school, on October 1, 1867, Mansfield had its new school, and during that first year, sixty-three students attended.

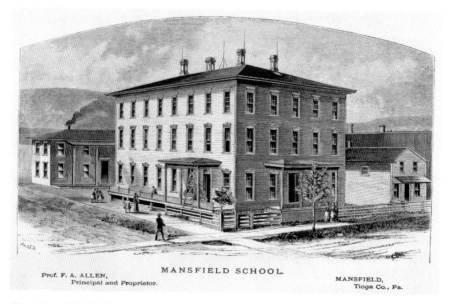

MANSFIELD SCHOOL.

Prof. F. A. ALLEN,
Principal and Proprietor.

MANSFIELD,
Tioga Co., Pa.

Above: Mansfield Soldiers' Orphan School. *Library of Congress.*

Opposite: Mansfield Soldiers' Orphan School marker. *Craig Swain, November 27, 2005, and www.hmdb.org.*

The first building was an empty store, which wasn't ideal for both home and school. Eventually, a larger building was purchased and enlarged to accommodate more than two hundred people.

The task of organizing this school was not without its challenges. Unlike a community school, the students, teachers and other staff were strangers to one another. In some instances, the teachers were senior students from the normal school.

By 1870, however, five separate grades had been established, with one teacher for each grade. About forty students were assigned to each grade, with instruction in language, mathematics and science.

In 1872, a farm of 150 acres outside of town was purchased. This provided employment and instruction for boys, who worked two hours a day. Girls were taught housework and sewing.[279]

Over the years, the local newspapers printed information on the school's former students. In 1877, Murray Vancise of Mansfield received an appointment as a telegraph operator and bookkeeper at the Elmira Reformatory. It was noted that he was a graduate of the Mansfield Soldiers' Orphan School and that he was "thoroughly competent and large enough physically to belong to the Prussian life guards."[280]

In 1878, John Matthews, a graduate of the Mansfield school, was appointed to West Point from Mansfield's Congressional district.[281] At the time, he was teaching at the normal school. John had been enrolled at the school with his twin brother, James Matthews. In 1938, in their eightieth year, James, who was living in Scranton, and John, who was living in Elmira, attended a reunion of the Mansfield Solders' Orphan School in Mansfield.[282]

Fred Wilcox, another Mansfield Soldiers' Orphan School student, went on to graduate from the Hahnemann Medical College in Philadelphia in 1886 and immediately entered the residency program of the Homoeopathic Hospital in Pittsburgh.[283]

There were classmates who married. Edwin Goodrich Watts, who in August 1927 was living in Chicago, and Nellie Mae Clark, of Colorado Springs, Colorado, took their vows of marriage at St. Andrew's Episcopal Church at Tioga, the same place where they were both confirmed when they were sixteen and seventeen years old.[284]

Mrs. Lucy Warren Rockwell was a student at the Mansfield Soldiers' Orphan School, later attending the Mansfield Normal School, where she became a teacher. Her father, William W. Warren, from Bradford County, died in service at Petersburg, Virginia. She joined her grandmother in Tioga County at the age of six.[285]

In August 1889, the Commonwealth made the decision to begin closing a number of schools around the state, one of those being the school in Mansfield. The orphans were redistributed to other locations. In an article in the local newspaper, it reported that the *Philadelphia Inquirer* commented that the schools were a system of farming out helpless orphans to enrich selfish people at the expense of the comfort, health and even lives of the children, that too much money had been appropriated by the state for the maintenance of the children. The article went on to note, however, that as far as was known, there were never any complaints made against the management of the Mansfield school and that the children were well clothed, well fed and treated to the satisfaction of the inspectors and state authorities. The attendance at the Mansfield school averaged 175 to 200 children, with the state paying $150 for the clothing, maintenance and tuition of each child. In 1888, the state paid the school $26,658.55. The paper noted that some people reasoned, "If any of the soldiers' orphans' schools are to be discontinued, why not close them all while we are about it? A child made an orphan during the war is certainly beyond school age now—being at least twenty-four years of age. While it was a noble charity in the beginning, certain of the schools have been nothing but jobs at the expense of the state in more recent years. Some people could not see why it was not our duty to educate, clothe and feed the grandchildren and great grandchildren of our dead soldiers, if we were bound to extend the orphan schools beyond a reasonable period after the close of the war."[286]

CIVIL WAR DEATH TOLL
AND POST-TRAUMATIC STRESS DISORDER

The traditional estimate has become iconic. It's been quoted for the last hundred years or more. If you go with that total for a minute—620,000— the number of men dying in the Civil War is more than all other American wars from the American Revolution through the Korean War combined. And consider that the American population in 1860 was about 31 million people, or about one-tenth of the size it is today. If the war were fought today, the number of deaths would total 6.2 million.[287]

In December 2011, J. David Hacker, a professor of history at SUNY– Binghamton, made headlines with a study published in the journal *Civil War History*. Over the years, estimates have been made that 620,000 people died in the Civil War, both Union and Confederate soldiers. Hacker claimed that the death toll could be as high as 750,000 or even 850,000. Hacker made his claim by studying census data from 1850 to 1880. He contends that deaths from disease or war-related injuries were never officially counted.

Hacker deemed that the Union and the Confederate States of America were focused on personnel records of men participating in the war. The governments were keeping records to determine field strengths and not in counting the dead.

Following the conflict, the War Department tried to get a direct count from muster-out rolls and established a number of Union soldiers who died: 300,000. That number was soon replaced with a higher number, 360,000, which was established when the widows and orphans started applying for pensions. Confederate records were destroyed, but decades after the war, an estimate of 94,000 Confederate deaths were projected.

Assuming, however, that Confederate men died at the same rate of disease and other noncombat causes as Union men did, the combined total was set at 620,000.

Early census tabulators did not have the tools to verify census tallies. Hacker examined age groups across census records and created a database using modern computers, following age groups—as an example, people 0–9 years old in 1850 are 10–19 years old in 1860, 20–29 in 1870 and 30–39 in 1880. While immigration could affect the figures, Hacker limited his count to native-born persons.[288]

Asked how Civil War deaths affected the country, Hacker contends that "the death rate—how many people died as a percentage of the population—is a better statistic than the absolute death toll. If we had the same death rate today as we had during the Civil War, we would be expecting 7.5 million deaths, which is staggering. And the South suffered disproportionately. We've long known that. My estimates indicate that more than twenty percent of the men ages 20–24 in 1860 who were born in the South died as a result of the war. A huge proportion of Southern women remained widowed in 1880. The loss of men in their prime affects more than marriage. We know that the Southern economy struggled for a long time."[289]

"Post-traumatic stress disorder," or PTSD, was a term that came into use following the Vietnam War. Recent research reveals that war-induced psychological trauma in American soldiers, which was first diagnosed during World War I as "shell shock" or "war neuroses," also affected American Civil War soldiers.[290] "We've tended to see soldiers in the 1860s as stoic and heroic—monuments to duty, honor and sacrifice. The men were bred on Victorian notions of manliness and courage."[291]

The participants in the Civil War faced factors unique to that era. The companies of soldiers in the Civil War were formed locally. The soldiers were likely to be relatives or men who had known one another for years. Witnessing a neighbor or brother killed in a horrific manner had a personal impact.[292]

While the circumstances of the Civil War were very different from modern warfare, the men who served suffered the same fates as many veterans of more recent wars: mental breakdowns, paranoia, suicidal behavior and more.[293]

Soldiers in the Civil War didn't travel to a foreign country to fight. Many of them were farm boys in their teens or early twenties who had never ventured far from family. Enlistments lasted three years. These conditions contributed to what Civil War doctors called "nostalgia," an old term for despair and homesickness. The recommended treatment was drilling and shaming of the soldiers, or "the excitement of an active campaign, combat."[294]

Men who showed what today would be war-related anxieties were thought to have character flaws or underlying physical problems. "Constricted breath and palpitations were known as 'soldier's heart' or 'irritable heart' and was blamed on exertion or knapsack straps drawn too tightly across soldiers' chests."[295]

In the 1860s, most troops fought on foot, marching in tight formation and firing at close range. Often in large-scale battles, they were armed with more accurate and deadly rifles and improved cannons. Bullets caused more than 90 percent of the bloodshed. Units were "cut down en masse, showering survivors with the blood, brains and body parts of their comrades."[296] The battles were horrific, and soldiers described landscapes strewn with so many bodies that "one could cross over them without touching the ground."[297]

"We've tended to see soldiers in the 1860s as stoic and heroic—monuments to duty, honor and sacrifice," said Lesley Gordon, editor of *Civil War History*, a leading academic journal. "It's taken a long time to recognize all the soldiers who came home broken by war, just as men and women do today."[298]

Part V

NOT TO BE FORGOTTEN

FACT OR FICTION?:
THE LOST CIVIL WAR GOLD SHIPMENT

There is a legend told in *A History of Elk County, Pennsylvania, 1981* by Alice Wessman, published by the Elk County Historical Society, about a missing Civil War gold shipment that has intrigued treasure hunters for more than one hundred years, and as recently as 2018, it was the subject of an actual search in Elk County by the Federal Bureau of Investigation and Department of Conservation and Natural Resources.

Under the heading "Thar's Gold in Them Thar Hills?," a historian related a tale of a gold shipment arriving outside of Ridgway, the county seat of Elk County, in June 1863, when a caravan of wagons and armed horsemen made their way up a Clarion River trail to a clearing, where they rested for the night. The caravan was made up of two heavy canvas-covered freight wagons and a smaller covered wagon known to the army as an ambulance. There were four mules, three drivers and eight men on horseback. According to the historian, "Concealed beneath false bottoms of the large wagons were twenty-six black painted ingots or bars of partly refined gold, each weighing fifty pounds and worth about $10,000 each."[299] Supposedly, the gold was being transported from Pittsburgh to Philadelphia, where it was intended for the federal mint. Concerned about guerrilla attacks on railroads in southern Pennsylvania, a secret route through Elk County was devised.

Gold ingots. *Wikimedia Commons.*

The main characters in this story were its commander, Lieutenant Castleton; Sergeant Mike O'Rourke; and another man only identified as Connors. The names of the others who took part in the caravan were not revealed.

Castleton was said to have been born into a famous military family; however, his combat career was ended by a hip wound, and he suffered from malaria. O'Rourke was "rough and tough and wanted by the police for several murderous river port brawls....He possessed a natural talent for leadership and shrewdness that Castleton lacked."[300] Connors was just plain "sullen, mean and unfriendly and had been wounded in combat."[301]

Castleton and O'Rourke, riding together into Ridgway, found that they were not welcome. Visiting a tavern, the two men were accused of being recruiters and drafters by some of the citizens. As noted in an earlier chapter, the draft was not popular. A fight broke out, and the two escaped. The next day, wisely detouring around Ridgway, the caravan headed for St. Marys, along what is today's State Route 120, arriving two days later.

In St. Marys, they located a map made in 1842 by a survey crew of what was described as "Wild Cat Country," showing a possible road branching off about ten miles east of St. Marys, going over the mountains and following a stream to the Sinnemahoning Creek. Deciding to follow this route, apparently the caravan made some wrong turns and got lost.

Castleton was weak from fever, and the rest of the party was exhausted. After discussion, it was decided that Connors would take two men and start out on foot southeast toward the village of Sinnemahoning to get help. Castleton and the five other men would transfer the gold from the wagons to saddles on the pack mules, and the men and mules would travel south. Before Connors left, Castleton gave him a written report summarizing the journey to that point and "a Federal Army order authorizing Connors to requisition men and supplies for the party's aid."[302] Connors later reported that when he left, Castleton and O'Rourke were arguing whether they should transport all of the gold on the mules or bury part of it.

Connors returned ten days later with a rescue party from Lock Haven; however, all they found was the abandoned wagons. It appeared that the main party split up, and after the rescuers searched for several days, they returned to Lock Haven without the lost men or the gold.

The War Department in Washington was notified, and a court of inquiry was held in Clearfield charging Castleton and O'Rourke with treason and theft; however, due to the status of Castleton's military family, charges were suspended pending investigation.

The Pinkerton Agency, being the main source of army intelligence at that time, was given the assignment of locating the lost gold and the men who had disappeared. Working in secrecy, the Pinkerton men took on the personas of prospectors or lumbermen to avoid detection by the locals as they searched the Bennett's Branch of the Sinnemahoning Creek as far west as St. Marys.[303]

What they found in 1865 was meager evidence: two and a half gold ingots buried under a pine stump about four miles from the spot where the wagons had been abandoned. To the experienced detectives, this indicated theft and a division of the gold.

In 1866, other Pinkerton detectives located one of the army mules. The mule, which carried the army brand, was found, according to the man in possession at the time, wandering in the woods.[304]

In 1876, when the Elk-Cameron County boundary line was resurveyed, surveyors found bones of three to five skeletons near a spring head near Dent's Run, about seven miles from where the wagons had been abandoned.

Fast-forward to 2018. Finders Keepers, a local lost treasure recovery service, maintains that it found the lost gold shipment in an area of Dents

Run Road in Benezette Township, Elk County, in 2012 and that federal law kept the group from digging for it. In March 2018, the *DuBois Courier-Express* carried a story, along with a photo, of where FBI agents set up to search for the gold. The *Courier* also reported that an FBI spokeswoman on site said that "agents were conducting court authorized law enforcement activity."[305]

The FBI claimed that it found nothing. The treasure hunters are asking for proof. Finders Keepers hired the services of an attorney to determine the results of the FBI search in the area where the service believes the lost gold was found. The attorney claims that the FBI has dragged its feet on the treasurer hunter's Freedom of Information Act request for records. "The FBI initially claimed it had no files about the investigation. Then, after the Justice Department ordered a more thorough review, the FBI said its records were exempt from public disclosure. Finally, in the wake of the treasure hunters' appeal, the FBI said it had located 2,300 pages of records and 17 video files that it could potentially turn over—but that it would take years to do so."[306]

On April 19, 2022, a local television station reported that a federal judge ordered the FBI to speed up the release of records. According to the report, "The FBI must turn over one thousand pages of records per month, starting in thirty days, and the first batch of records must include a key report sought by Finders Keepers," U.S. District Judge Amit P. Metah ordered.[307] Fact or fiction? Time will tell.

JOHN WILKES BOOTH, PENNSYLVANIA OILMAN

Most people know something of the man who killed President Abraham Lincoln on the night of April 14, 1865. Born in 1838, John Wilkes Booth, along with his brother Edwin, was an actor on the American stage. A southerner by birth, Booth had an almost fanatical devotion to the cause of the Confederacy, and this pushed him to commit the act of murder.

What may surprise many is that Booth had a connection to the Wilds, having traveled through the region to reach Venango County, where he had investments in oil. In a book titled *John Wilkes Booth—Oilman* by Ernest C. Miller, the author outlined Booth's interest in investments, noting his friendship with a banker from Boston who was familiar with the real estate market and who assisted Booth in his efforts. Apparently looking ahead to a time when he was no longer on the stage, these investments may have provided him with some modest income. In January 1864, Booth was on

John Wilkes Booth. *Wikimedia Commons.*

the stage at Ben DeBar's St. Louis Theater. During this time, Booth was persuaded to visit the Pennsylvania oil region. Accompanied by two acquaintances from Cleveland, the three made their way to Franklin, where there was much excitement about the oil business. Booth and his partners, having surveyed the area, formed an oil company known as the Dramatic Oil Company. According to Miller, there is no record of Dramatic Oil Company in the Prothonotary's Office of Venango County, noting that "many partnerships came into being without legal papers either being prepared or filed."[308] The property selected was three and a half acres bordering on the Allegheny River. The company hired an experienced driller, and Booth returned to the stage in New Orleans in March of that year.

Returning to Franklin for most of the summer of 1864 to look after his oil interests, Booth lived in a boardinghouse owned by Mrs. Sarah Webber. The house, which dated back to 1842, was eventually purchased by the Elk Lodge and later removed.

There are several accounts of Booth's time in Franklin. In an article published in the *News-Herald* in 1971, Irwin Ross wrote "The Man No One Knew"[309] for the VFW magazine. According to the news article, the person Ross was writing about was unnamed throughout most of his writing. However, Ross did offer a description: "Of medium height, eyes black and expressive, his hair was always carefully brushed and his black moustache groomed with equal care. It was his full, rich voice, however, that most people remembered. That, and his little acts of kindness."[310]

Ross went on to recount that the "Man No One Knew" "furnished his rooms with good pieces, hung fine paintings and received express shipments of good books. His closets were filled with expensive clothing."[311]

According to Ross, Booth was known to be moody, and when asked about his religion, he stated, "I have no settled beliefs," and after saying that, "he quoted the Sermon on the Mount."[312]

Booth also had a temper and beat a teamster for cruel treatment of a horse, but he was apparently adored by a young boy known as "Little Joe Watson," son of a neighbor of Mrs. Webber's.

There is speculation about the oil business Booth was engaged in, with some saying that he made money, while others believe he went broke. Whatever the case, he eventually left Franklin and returned to the stage.

Booth was not forgotten in the region. In 1890, Michael McDermott wrote to the editor of the *Potter Enterprise*, Coudersport, Pennsylvania, of his remembrances of Booth:

> *He [President Lincoln] was a great favorite of mine, as also was John Wilkes Booth, who was my personal friend. Booth often came to Franklin, Venango Co., where he was interested in the oil business with Tom Mears of Cleveland as a partner. Tom Mears and I were walking down Liberty Street on the morning of April 15th, 1865, when the first dispatch came to town announcing the assassination of President Lincoln. The assassin's name was not given in the dispatch. We walked back and forth a while longer, and then I said: "Tom, if the President has been killed, it is John W. Booth that did it." He stopped and I'll never forget the look he gave me, and asked why I made such a remark. I answered that I had cause for saying so; that Booth made a remark in my company, about Lincoln, the year before, which I did not like. "Mack" he said, "if that should be the case, I would be a ruined man." In half an hour the second dispatch, announcing the name of J. Booth as the assassin. Tom Mears would have dropped to the sidewalk but for my help.*[313]

For years after Booth's death, there were theories that he was not the person killed on that Maryland farm, as reported in the news; did he make his way out of the country following the killing of Lincoln? As late as 1937, the *News-Herald* in Franklin carried a story that Booth had escaped, an article from Glen Rose, Texas, titled "Booth's Ghost Legend Revived: Story Once Again Told of Man Who Claimed to Be Slayer of Abraham Lincoln":

> *Abraham Lincoln's birthday anniversary revived the legend of the "ghost" of his slayer, John Wilkes Booth, whom many old-timers believe lived here after assassinating the beloved Civil War President.*
>
> *The records of Booth were closed shortly after Lincoln's death when Federal troops supposedly trapped the assassin in a burning barn near Washington. But to many persons here and in nearby Granbury, John Wilkes Booth was the dapper saloon-keeper who came from the east about 1870 and took his own life in Enid, Okla. in 1903.*
>
> *Those who lived in this frontier village at the time wondered why an easterner of apparent culture would come to Glen Rose to run a saloon. When*

he moved to Granbury in 1872 to continue in the same business, the secret went with him. The mystery was deepened because of the sword wound he carried over one eye, because his limp was so great from a crooked ankle that he walked with a cane, and because he quoted Shakespeare profusely.

At Granbury, the stranger—who called himself "John St. Helen"—became friendly with Attorney Finis Bates. One day St. Helen became violently ill and when told he had only a short time to live, he summoned Bates to his bedside. "I have some personal papers and a photograph of myself," the stranger told Bates. "When I'm gone, I want you to send them to my brother in New York—Edwin Booth, the actor. Perhaps you've already guessed it, but I'm John Wilkes Booth."

St. Helen recovered, lived in Granbury several years, and acquaintances called him "John Wilkes Booth."[314]

The article concluded by stating that by 1900, he had disappeared and was not heard of again until 1903, when he committed suicide in an Enid, Oklahoma hotel. Other stories about Booth claimed that he left the country and went to India.

Ely Parker, a Seneca Indian

General Grant introduced to Lee the officers of the Union Army who were in the room....Lee greeted each staff officer and then being introduced to Colonel Parker who was busy with his papers, he looked at him searchingly....Parker being a full-blood Indian. When Lee saw his swarthy features, he looked at him with evident surprise and his eyes rested on him for several seconds. What was passing in his mind no one knew, but the natural surmise is that he first mistook Parker for a negro.... "After Lee had stared at me for a moment," said Parker, "he extended his hand and said, 'I am glad to see one real American here.' I shook his hand and said, 'We are all Americans.'"[315]

Pennsylvania has a rich Native American heritage, with several distinct peoples having lived in the state, including the Delawares or Lenni-Lenape; the Susquehannocks; the Monongahela people; the Eries; and, more recently, the Iroquois.[316]

One of the tribes in the Iroquois Federation was the Seneca tribe. In modern times, within the region of the Wilds, that tribe is well known because of the history of its chief Cornplanter, who settled in what is now Warren County. Following the American Revolution in which the Seneca, including Cornplanter, sided with the British, Cornplanter extended a conciliatory response to the Pennsylvania government following the Harmar Treaty in 1789. In thanks, the Pennsylvania government gave him three land grants: one near West Hickory, another near Oil City and the third, six hundred acres, south of the New York state line in Warren County. Selling the first two, Cornplanter retained the third tract, which included his own

Ely Parker. *Wikimedia Commons.*

town, Jenuchshadega, and two islands in the Allegheny River. These lands vanished under the waters of a flood-control dam completed in 1964, the Kinzua Dam.[317] At the time of the building of the dam, few of Cornplanter's descendants lived on the land grant, although many considered it a home and place of refuge.[318]

The Seneca Nation of Indians currently has a total enrolled population of nearly eight thousand citizens. The historical Seneca occupied territory throughout the Finger Lakes area in Central New York and in the Genesee Valley in Western New York.[319] Near the Pennsylvania border, twenty miles north of Bradford, McKean County, the city of Salamanca, New York, within reservation lands, has a population of about six thousand, with 35 percent being Native American.[320]

Ely Parker, a Seneca Indian, was born at Tonawanda, New York, in 1828. Born as Hasanoanda or "Leading Name," shortly after birth he became known as Ely Samuel Parker—Parker was the "white" name his family was known by and Ely was a name of a Baptist missionary. In adulthood, he became known as Donehogawa, "The Door Keeper," or more specifically as the title of the last national sachem in the role of Iroquois sachems, "The Keeper of the Western Door."[321]

About four months before the birth of her son, his mother, Elizabeth, had a strange dream. It made such an impression on her that Elizabeth consulted a Seneca dream interpreter. Her dream took place in the winter at the Buffalo Reservation near the Granger farm. Strangely, in the dream, the sky opened from the middle, and although it was snowing, she saw a rainbow in the middle. From one side of the rainbow, signs with letters similar to those seen over white men's stores were suspended from the rainbow. The dream interpreter, a man, told her that it was a prophecy and added, "A son will be born to you who will be distinguished among his nation as a peacemaker; he will become a white man as well as an Indian. He will be a wise white man, but will never desert his Indian people, nor 'lay down his horns' [sachem's title] as a great chief, his name will reach from the east to the west, the north to the south, as great among his Indian family and pale-faces. His sun will rise on Indian land and set on white man's land. Yet the ancient land of his ancestors will fold him in death."[322]

The year 1857 was the beginning of the fulfillment of this prophecy. Parker, who was working as a superintendent of construction for a customhouse and a marine hospital in Galena, Illinois, became acquainted with the clerk in the harness store. The two had long talks, with the clerk doing most of the talking. The harness shop clerk who befriended him was Ulysses S. Grant.[323]

Parker started school at the Baptist Mission School at Tonawanda.[324] His parents believed in education for their children, and he attended Rensselaer Polytechnic Institute, choosing a career in engineering.[325] But that was not his first career choice. A man of many interests, he first turned his attention to the study of law, spending three years reading law, drawing up forms, preparing arguments and listening to court proceedings as a student in the law office of Angel and Rice in Ellicottville, Cattaraugus County, New York. Competent in every requirement, Parker nonetheless learned that he would not be admitted to the bar. A Supreme Court decision had ruled that only a white, male American citizen could sit for the exam. He could not be admitted because he was neither white nor a citizen of the country, according to the laws at that time.[326]

When the first rumors of war were heard, Parker was interested in serving his country. At the time, he was conducting engineering work on the levees of the Mississippi and was advised to stay on, as "the war would last for only a few months at most. In the meantime, his friend, Grant, recruited a regiment and was later ordered to the front."[327]

In 1862, with the war dragging on, Parker decided to resign his position to go home to Tonawanda to ask his father's consent to enlist in the army. "Father," he said in his native tongue, "I think I ought to fight for my country just as you did years ago. I want you to let me go." His father said he would think it over and let him know the next day.[328] The next day, Parker showed his father an article from *Harper's Weekly* that showed a photo of army officers and a drawing of a battle scene. His father placed his finger on the photo, saying, "Here is the man who will be the great general who shall lead his army to victory. You follow him and you will be a great war captain, too." The man in the photo was Ulysses Grant.[329]

With the blessing of his father and speeches made in his honor by his people, they sent him on to the governor of New York. Arriving in Albany with high hopes, he went to the governor, noting his experiences as an engineer. The governor looked at him and said that he had no place for him.[330]

Qualified to be an army engineer and not easily discouraged, Parker went from Rochester to Washington, D.C., to offer his services to the War Department, meeting in person with Secretary William H. Seward. "Mr. Seward said to me that the struggle in which I wished to assist was an affair between white men and one in which the Indian was not called to act. 'This fight must be settled by white men alone. Go home. Cultivate your farm and we will settle our own troubles without any Indian aid.'"[331]

Parker returned home to cultivate his land. Knowing that soldiers needed food, he plowed his land out of a sense of patriotism. And yet, following the news of Grant's actions, he also reflected on the fact that three hundred of his kinsmen were fighting in the war. He ignored unkind remarks such as, "He can't be much of a man to be refused by the Army." Then, one afternoon, a horse carrying a soldier came galloping down the road. The horse stopped beside Parker, and the soldier handed Parker a paper that was stamped with the red seal of the War Department. Parker had received an officer's commission in the U.S. Army. It is said to have been signed by President Lincoln, transmitted through the secretary of war. He was given the rank of captain. Parker later wrote, "It seemed odd that an Indian was now desired and that the Government wished to confer honors for which I had not served an apprenticeship, nor even asked." The commission was formally accepted on June 4, 1863. His people celebrated with a feast in his honor.[332]

Apparently, Parker had contacted his old friend Ulysses Grant directly. Grant was suffering from a shortage of engineers, and thus Parker received his commission. He was with Grant and other officers through many "hot" campaigns. Eventually, he became military secretary to Grant. Much of Grant's correspondence was transcribed by Parker, and during a time of great pressure, Grant trusted him to prepare important letters, orders and reports for Grant's signature.[333]

At Lee's surrender at Appomattox in April 1865, Parker was present and helped draft the surrender documents. The final documents were completed by Parker, as it was noted, "His handwriting presented a better appearance."[334]

The surrender of Lee, Appomattox Court House, Virginia, April 9, 1865. *Library of Congress.*

Parker was appointed brevet brigadier general of U.S. Volunteers by Grant "[f]or gallant and meritorious services during the surrender of the insurgent army under General Robert E. Lee." The appointment was dated April 9, 1865, the date of Lee's surrender.[335] After Grant took office as president in March 1869, he appointed Parker commissioner of Indian affairs, the first Native American to hold that post.[336]

Twenty-nine years after Ely Parker died, the Indian Citizenship Act, which granted citizenship to Native Americans, was passed by Congress on June 2, 1924.[337]

Part VI

OLD-TIME RECIPES

Kate Maria Hyde Hall and the *Ridgway Cook Book*

Kate Maria Hyde was born in Horton Township, Elk County, Pennsylvania, on November 22, 1853, the daughter of Joseph Smith Hyde and Jane Gillis Hyde. Her grandfather Enos Gillis was one of the early settlers in Ridgway. Kate was a child when the Civil War broke out.

Her father was a self-made man who was born in New Hampshire. He first arrived in Caledonia, Jay Township, Elk County, in 1837. Plagued by illness and without money, he moved on to Ridgway, taking a job with Enos Gillis working in the woods. After a period of time, he left Ridgway for about a year to work in Wisconsin. Once again, ill and discouraged, he returned to Ridgway, again working in the woods.[338]

Hyde became interested in Jane Gillis, the daughter of Enos Gillis, his employer. Marrying her on July 25, 1842, he eventually took over operating his father-in-law's mill. As he accumulated wealth, he built a home on Main Street and East Avenue, opening a store in the residence. As his wealth grew, he purchased multiple tracts of timberland, erecting sawmills to handle the wood. Eventually, Hyde became the largest manufacturer of lumber in the country.[339]

In the 1860s, Mr. Hyde moved his family to Ohio for better educational opportunities. In 1864, his wife, Jane, died while living there, and he returned the family to Ridgway.

Hyde went on to erect a large planning mill. He built the Hotel Hyde in downtown Ridgway, and he and a former manager of his one of plants

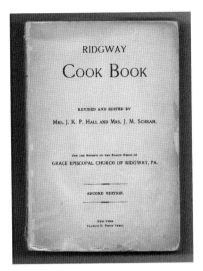

RIDGWAY

COOK BOOK

REVISED AND EDITED BY
MRS. J. K. P. HALL AND MRS. J. M. SCHRAM.

FOR THE BENEFIT OF THE PARISH GUILD OF
GRACE EPISCOPAL CHURCH OF RIDGWAY, PA.

SECOND EDITION.

NEW YORK
FRANKLIN H. PUGH PRESS.

Ridgway Cook Book. Kathy Myers.

formed the Hyde-Murphy Company in 1901, which is remembered to this day for its fine woodworking, evident in many of the homes in Ridgway as well as other places, including our nation's capital.[340]

Ridgway, as with other communities in the Wilds, was caught up in the passion of responding to the Civil War. Kate experienced that response by the citizens of Ridgway. One such person who was involved in the Civil War was her cousin James H. Gillis. The son of James L. Gillis and nephew of Kate's grandfather Enos Gillis, James left his Montmorenci farm home at age seventeen to enter the U.S. Naval Academy at Annapolis, receiving his commission in 1855. During the Civil War, at the Battle of Mobile Bay, he commanded a warship. Sunk by a torpedo, James kept firing his guns until the gundeck was submerged. He was cited for bravery on more than one occasion.[341]

Another local man, John A. Boyle, was a minister and lawyer. In 1856, he purchased the *Elk Reporter* and published a newspaper with the assistance of his two sons. He lived on West Main Street near the Gillis store. During the Civil War, he rose to the rank of major. Boyle was killed in action during a battle at Wauhatchie, Tennessee, on October 29, 1863. He held the highest rank of any local soldier to be killed in the conflict.[342]

Ridgway saw action in the war in another way. Dr. J.S. Bardwell, from Warren, was appointed the local surgeon of the invalid corps in January 1865. At that time, there were fifty-six wounded soldiers housed in the original old courthouse. In two months, another group arrived. They were kept in a schoolhouse across the Clarion River. All of the men recovered and were discharged.[343]

Kate's mother was known as an extremely kind person, and that trait appears to have rubbed off on Kate, who is well known for her philanthropy in Ridgway. In 1875, she married James Knox Polk Hall at the Grace Episcopal Church in Ridgway. She and her husband built various homes in town that are standing today, and they were the owners of Rough and Ready Farm, an estate that had been part of her father's early lumbering activities.

Kate carried on many good works in Ridgway, organizing the building of the Elk County General Hospital in 1901. She was founder and president of the Village Improvement Association and president of the Ridgway Public Library and the Progress Club, member of the Humane Society and the Audubon Society of Ridgway and a lifelong member of the Grace Episcopal Church.[344]

Mrs. Hall, along with Mrs. J.M. Schram, published a second edition of *Ridgway Cook Book* for the benefit of the Parish Guild of Grace Episcopal Church of Ridgway Pennsylvania.[345] Mrs. Hall owned the copyright.

Along with Mrs. Hall, Mrs. Schram was also a young girl during the Civil War. Others who contributed to the book were children during the war and, in the case of some, children of Civil War soldiers. How much did those years influence the selection of recipes in the book? One cannot say. A few of the old-time recipes in the *Ridgway Cook Book* are shared here.

Smear Kase

Scald sour milk, as soon as it has thickened, with one pint of boiling water to a gallon of milk. Stir until the curd commences to separate from the whey. Drain through cheese cloth until every particle of the whey is out. Mash fine or pass through a sieve. Add a teacup of good, sweet cream to every pint of curd and season to taste with pepper and salt.

For cheese balls to serve with salad, use half the quantity of cream and mold into balls like butter balls. Chopped chives, olives or nuts are a pleasant addition.—Mrs. J.K.P. Hall [346]

This is cottage cheese or a spreadable cheese, from the German word *schmierkase* or from the Pennsylvania Amish word *smearcase*.

Corn Soup

One can of corn, two cups of milk, two tablespoonfuls of flour, pepper and salt, two cups of boiling water, one tablespoonful of butter, one egg.

Drain the liquor from the corn, chop fine, add boiling water and cook one hour. Rub through a colander and return to the fire. Rub butter and flour together, add to hot milk, then the beaten egg. Stir this into the corn and serve hot.—Mrs. Henry Whiting [347]

Potato Croquettes

Three cups mashed potatoes, one tablespoonful butter, yolks of two eggs, salt, pepper, parsley, onion. Grate in the yellow rind of a lemon. Grate onion. Mix together, beat till light, make in rolls dipped in beaten white of egg, put in bread crumbs, fry in hot fat a nice brown.—Mary E. Garritt [348]

Toad in the Hole

This is a good English dish, despite its unpleasant name. One pound round steak, one pint of milk, one cup of flour, one egg, salt and pepper. Cut the steak into small pieces. Beat the egg very slightly; add the milk, then half a teaspoonful of salt. Pour upon the flour gradually, beating very light and smooth. Butter a two-quart dish, put in the meat, season well and pour over it the batter. Bake one hour in a moderate oven. Serve hot. This dish can be made with lamb in place of steak. Cooked meat can be used, but fresh is better.—Cora Gifford [349]

Roast Venison

Have the butcher remove the bones from two or three ribs of venison, so that it can be easily rolled. Lay in a slice of pork, roll tightly and bind with twine, dredge with flour, pepper and salt and cook until well done. Serve with spiced gooseberries.—Mrs. Anna Doane [350]

Orange Custard

Three eggs, one cupful of sugar, one tablespoonful of butter, two tablespoonfuls of powdered sugar, one cupful of milk, one orange, juice only. Beat yolks of eggs to a cream, with butter and sugar; add milk, orange juice, and beaten white of one egg. Fill custard cups two-thirds full, place in pan of water, and bake until custard sets. Beat whites of two eggs with sugar and put one tablespoonful on top of each cup and brown delicately.— Mr. C.E. Rogers [351]

Soft Ginger Cookies

One cupful of molasses, one cupful of brown sugar, one half cupful of lukewarm water, one cupful of butter, scant, one egg, one teaspoonful of ginger, one teaspoonful of soda, one nutmeg. Roll very soft and bake in a quick oven.—Mrs. Lizzie Dietz [352]

Chocolate Caramels

One pound of brown sugar, one forth pound of chocolate, one half cupful of milk or cream, one-half cupful of butter, one-half cupful of molasses, one cupful of chopped cream nuts, one teaspoonful of vanilla. Cook all the ingredient together excepting the vanilla and the nuts. When the temperature is two hundred fifty-four degrees Fahr, remove from the range, and add the nuts and vanilla, and pour immediately into a shallow pan seven by eleven inches, which has been well buttered. If they are not soft but sugared, add a little cream or milk, and cook again to the same temperature. If not hard enough cook again. English walnuts may be used.—Maud L. Hirons [353]

CONCLUSION

The consciousness of duty was pervasive in Victorian America. Union volunteers filled their letters and diaries with such phrases as "I went from a sense of duty"; if my three-months regiment reenlists for three years "it would be my duty to go"; I must sacrifice personal feelings and inclinations "to my duty in the hour of danger"; in enlisting, "I performed but a simple duty—a duty to my country and myself to give up life if need be in this battle for freedom and right, opposed to slavery and wrong." [354]

As we contemplated in the introduction, are we now living in the most divisive times in our country's history? The answer to that question falls to each reader to decide based on their own experiences and observations of life in this country today.

The research for this book has shown that we were a deeply divided nation in the years leading up to the Civil War. Issues of slavery and states' rights caused bitterness in both the North and the South.

Abolitionists were determined to end slavery in this country, while Copperheads were working for the defeat of the Union. The draft, which in my lifetime has been commonplace, was very unpopular.

There were "ordinary" people living in the Wilds who may have never known a slave or a plantation owner. But they were moved into action, not so much because of their convictions against slavery but rather to preserve the Union. The surrender of Fort Sumter was a call to battle. Throughout their years of service, however, soldiers became acquainted with the plight

of the slaves, and their thinking about slavery changed. As one private in a Pennsylvania regiment wrote in January 1862, "I thought I hated slavery as much as possible before I came here, but here, where I can see some of its workings, I am more than ever convinced of the cruelty and inhumanity of the system."[355]

The number of people involved in the Underground Railroad in the Wilds is remarkable. These people acted on their convictions, defying the federal government via actions they recognized were not legal, but they were determined to do what they could to help the slaves to freedom.

Because of the war, some families were torn apart by divorce, and many suffered financially. There were returning soldiers who were never whole again because of their wounds, with some dying at an early age. Today, it is recognized that Civil War soldiers also suffered from post-traumatic stress disorder, as have later generations of service men and women.

Out of necessity, women experienced a newfound independence that had not been known to those growing up in the Victorian age. Many became active participants in the conflict by becoming nurses; women organized drives to provide relief to soldiers in the form of food and clothing; and in some instances, women worked outside of the home to make ends meet. Eventually, these new freedoms led to the suffrage movement and an amendment, which failed, introduced to Congress in 1878. Eventually, the Nineteenth Amendment to the Constitution was adopted by Congress in 1919. When it was ratified in 1920, women gained the right to vote.

Top: Grand Army of the Republic reunion, Indiana, Pennsylvania, August 22, 1929. *Kathy Myers.*

Above: Bucktail reunion, Kane, Pennsylvania, August 30, 1884. *L. Tom Perry Special Collections, Harold B. Lee Library, Brigham Young University.*

Through the actions of the soldiers from the Wilds, along with many others, the Union prevailed. The Thirteenth Amendment to the Constitution, adopted in 1865, ended slavery in the United States.

Over the years, soldiers gathered to reminisce about their service during the war. Grand Army of the Republic (GAR) posts were very popular. "It quickly became the preeminent veterans' organization formed at the close of the Civil War. Membership reached its peak in 1890 when over four hundred thousand members were reported, with over seven thousand posts....The organization of the GAR was based upon three objectives: fraternity, charity and loyalty."[356] Posts were established throughout the Wilds region.

The Bucktail Regiment also held reunions after the war, with one such reunion depicted in a photo taken in Kane, Pennsylvania, the town founded by Thomas L. Kane, the organizer of the Bucktail Regiments. Today, in various locations in the Wilds and beyond, groups of Civil War reenactors gather to build rafts and sail down the Sinnemahoning Creek or shoot guns in mock battles, clothed in Civil War uniforms. They have been joined by women and children dressed in period costumes, and they have enjoyed performances of music from that era. Truly a reflection of the national and regional fascination with that period of American life.

The war resulted in the growth of the federal government, and the country was referred to in a new way: "Before 1861 the two words 'United States' were generally used as a plural noun, 'the United States are a republic.' After 1865, the United States became a singular noun."[357] The United States *is* a republic.

NOTES

Preface

1. Commonwealth of Pennsylvania, "State Symbols."

Part I

2. Pennsylvania Wilds, "About."
3. Ibid.
4. Ibid.
5. *Merriam-Webster*, "coming-of-age," www.merriam-webster.com/dictionary/coming-of-age.
6. *Jeffersonian Democrat*, "Summerless Year," 1.
7. Scott, *History of Jefferson County, Pennsylvania*, 43.
8. *History of the Counties of McKean, Elk, and Forest*, 53.
9. Ibid., 586.
10. Scott, *History of Jefferson County, Pennsylvania*, 63.
11. Ibid.
12. Ibid.
13. Meginness, *History of Lycoming County, Pennsylvania*, 273–74.
14. *History of the Counties of McKean, Elk, and Forest*, 112.
15. Ibid., 590.
16. Ibid., 862.
17. Scott, *History of Jefferson County, Pennsylvania*, 228.
18. Ibid.
19. *History of the Counties of McKean, Elk, and Forest*, 613.
20. Pennsylvania Department of Transportation, "St. James Episcopal Church."

21. Caldwell, *Caldwell's Atlas of Jefferson County, Pennsylvania*, 20.

22. Ibid., 21.

23. Pennsylvania State University, "Founding of a Land Grant University."

24. Lycoming College, "About."

25. Mansfield University Archived Catalogue, "History."

26. *Funk & Wagnalls New Encyclopedia*, "Civil War," 170.

27. Ibid., "James Monroe," 474.

28. *Britannica*, "Era of Good Feelings."

29. *Funk & Wagnalls New Encyclopedia*, "Civil War," 170.

30. Ibid., "Louisiana Purchase," 311–12.

31. National Archives and Records Administration, "Missouri Compromise (1820)."

32. *Funk & Wagnalls New Encyclopedia*, "Dred Scott Case," 168.

33. *Britannica*, "Fugitive Slave Acts."

34. *Funk & Wagnalls New Encyclopedia*, "Abolitionists," 150.

35. *National Geographic*, "Abolition and the Abolitionists."

36. Turner, "Slavery in Pennsylvania," 65.

37. Ibid., "Negro in Pennsylvania," 86.

38. *Tioga Eagle (Wellsboro, PA)*, "Fugitive Slave Bill," 4.

39. *Brookville (PA) Republican*, "Political Preachers," 2.

40. *Brookville (PA) Republican*, "New Publications," 2.

41. *Funk & Wagnalls New Encyclopedia*, "Knights of the Golden Circle," 422.

42. *Raftsman's Journal (Clearfield, PA)*, "Knights of the Golden Circle," 1.

43. *Raftsman's Journal (Clearfield, PA)*, "Can It Be?" 1.

44. *Brookville (PA) Republican*, "What Is the Reason?," 2.

45. *Wellsboro (PA) Gazette–Mansfield Advertiser*, "Select Poetry, Where Are the Copperheads?," 1.

46. *Brookville Jeffersonian*, "War Commenced," 3.

47. *Clearfield Republican*, "War Begun," 2.

48. *Britannica*, "Fort Sumter National Monument."

49. Ibid.

Part II

50. Pennsylvania Historic and Museum Commission, "Guide for Classroom Teachers."

51. Historical Marker Database, "Bucktail Monument."

52. Pennsylvania Historic and Museum Commission, "Forty-Second Regiment."

53. Kane Area Development Center, "History of Kane."

54. Grow, "Thomas L. Kane and Nineteenth-Century American Culture," 5.

55. *Kane Republican*, "Address of Robert Gray Taylor," 4.

56. Grow, "Thomas L. Kane and Nineteenth-Century American Culture," 8.

57. *Kane Republican*, "Address of Robert Gray Taylor."

58. McAllister, "Kane, Thomas Leiper."

59. Grow, "Thomas L. Kane and Nineteenth-Century American Culture," 11.

60. *Kane Republican*, "Address of Robert Gray Taylor."
61. Grow, "Thomas L. Kane and Nineteenth-Century American Culture," 12.
62. Ibid., 13.
63. Ibid.
64. *History of the Counties of McKean, Elk, and Forest*, 315.
65. Pennsylvania Historic and Museum Commission, "Forty-Second Regiment."
66. *Kane Republican*, "Seen from the Hilltop," 4.
67. Watson, "Last Survivors, Two Bucktails," 6.
68. Ibid.
69. Bates, *History of the Pennsylvania Volunteers*, 907.
70. Wessman, *History of Elk County*, 50.
71. Ibid.
72. "Deo Volente," a Latin phrase meaning "God Willing," from the Free Dictionary, www.thefreedictionary.com/DV.
73. Brigham Young University Library, Thomas L. Kane, letter to Elizabeth Wood Kane.
74. Kinzua Bridge Foundation, "History."
75. Kane Historic Preservation Society, "Chapel."
76. Wessman, *History of Elk County*, 87–89.
77. Howard, *History of the Bucktails*, 29.
78. Ibid., 10–11.
79. Ibid., 11.
80. Ibid., 11–12.
81. Ibid., 29.
82. Ibid.
83. *Kane Republican*, "Seen from the Hilltop," 4.
84. Wessman, *History of Elk County*, 280.
85. Kathy Myers, "Winslow Genealogy."
86. Wessman, *History of Elk County*, 291.
87. 1850, 1860 Federal Census.
88. Kathy Myers, "Winslow Genealogy."
89. Mount Zion Historical Society, "Remembering Lieutenant Colonel."
90. Ibid.
91. Ibid.
92. 1870 Federal Census.
93. Parsons Holton, *Winslow Memorial*, 998.
94. Aldrich, *History of Clearfield County, Pennsylvania*, 566.
95. *Cameron County Press*, "Another Bucktail Gone," 1.
96. *Pike County Dispatch*, "Died in Virginia," 1.
97. *History of the Counties of McKean, Elk, Cameron and Potter*, 843.
98. *Pike County Dispatch*, "Died in Virginia," 1.
99. 1850 Federal Census, Clinton County, Pennsylvania.
100. *History of the Counties of McKean, Elk, Cameron and Potter*, 848.
101. *Pike County Dispatch*, "Died in Virginia," 1.

102. *Kane Republican*, "Seen from the Hilltop," 4.
103. Howard, *History of the Bucktails*, 13.
104. Bates, *History of the Pennsylvania Volunteers*, 907.
105. *History of the Counties of McKean, Elk, Cameron and Potter*, 849.
106. *Elk County Advocate*, "You Voted for the Draft," 1.
107. History, "Congress Passes Civil War Conscription Act."
108. Ibid.
109. Schenck, *History of Warren County, Pennsylvania*, 165–66.
110. *Clearfield County*, "Best Place to Escape to in Pennsylvania."
111. Visit Clearfield County, "Bloody Knox."
112. Clara Barton Missing Soldiers Office Museum, "Clara Barton Biography."
113. Ibid.
114. *Jeffersonian Democrat*, "Death of Miss Kate M. Scott," 8.
115. Indiana State University Library, "Kate M. Scott's Sworn Statement."
116. Ibid.
117. Scott, *History of the One Hundred and Fifth Regiment*, 13.
118. *Jeffersonian Democrat*, "Death of Miss Kate M. Scott."
119. *Jeffersonian Democrat*, "Pennsylvania Memorial Home."
120. Death Certificate, June 1909, Ridgway, Elk County, Pennsylvania, Ancestry. com.
121. Wessman and Faust, *Sesquicentennial History of Ridgway, Pennsylvania*, 145.
122. Alexandria Archaeology Museum, "Union Hospitals in Alexandria."
123. Ibid.
124. Wessman and Faust, *Sesquicentennial History of Ridgway, Pennsylvania*, 145.
125. Ibid.
126. *Wellsboro (PA) Gazette–Mansfield Advertiser*, "She Was a Civil War Nurse," 6.
127. Ibid.
128. Ibid.
129. Ibid.

Part III

130. *The Progress*, "North Star Way Picked as Name," 11.
131. West, "North Star to Freedom."
132. History, "This Day in History."
133. Switala, *Underground Railroad in Pennsylvania*, 17.
134. Ibid., 29, 34, 38.
135. Ibid., 27, 111.
136. Wallace, *Indian Paths of Pennsylvania*, 155.
137. Donehoo, *History of the Indian Villages and Place Names*, 206.
138. Ibid.
139. Visit Central Pennsylvania, "Underground Railroad."
140. Beebe, *History of Potter County Pennsylvania*, 117.
141. Allegheny College, "Elihu Chadwick, Jr."

142. Ibid.
143. Waters, "Outdoor Adventures Expo."
144. Pennsylvania Historic and Museum Commission, "Governor Andrew Gregg Curtin."
145. Gosaloz, "Scholar Talks About Bellefonte's Underground Railroad," 1.
146. Visit Pennsylvania Great Outdoors, "Clarion County."
147. Davis, *History of Clarion County, Pennsylvania*, 125–26.
148. Ibid., 121–22.
149. *Clarion Democrat*, "Death of Benjamin Gardner," 5.
150. Aldrich, *History of Clearfield County, Pennsylvania*, 481.
151. Ibid.
152. Ibid., 481–82.
153. Ibid., 481.
154. Switala, *Underground Railroad in Pennsylvania*, 38.
155. Ibid.
156. Donehoo, *History of the Indian Villages and Place Names*, 243.
157. Ibid., 28.
158. Wallace, *Indian Paths of Pennsylvania*, 174.
159. Donehoo, *History of the Indian Villages and Place Names*, 274.
160. Susquehanna Greenway, "Riots Rumors and Stories."
161. Bernard, "Celebrate Black History."
162. Ibid.
163. Ibid.
164. Find A Grave, "Rev Joseph Nesbitt."
165. Bernard, "Celebrate Black History."
166. National Wild and Scenic Rivers System, "Clarion River, Pennsylvania."
167. Wessman, *History of Elk County*, 162.
168. Wessman and Faust, *Sesquicentennial History of Ridgway, Pennsylvania*, 11.
169. Switala, *Underground Railroad in Pennsylvania*, 27.
170. Wessman, *History of Elk County*, 119.
171. *Elk County Advocate*, "Notes," 3.
172. *Jeffersonian Democrat*, "Watch Story," 8.
173. Pennsylvania Great Outdoors Visitors Bureau, "Forest County."
174. U.S. Census Bureau, "QuickFacts: Forest County, Pennsylvania."
175. World Population Review, "Population of Counties in Pennsylvania (2023)."
176. *History of the Counties of McKean, Elk, and Forest*, 815.
177. McKnight, *Pioneer Outline History of Northwestern Pennsylvania*, 518.
178. Ibid., 521.
179. *History of the Counties of McKean, Elk, and Forest*, 836.
180. Historical Marker Database, "Marienville."
181. McKnight, *Pioneer Outline History of Northwestern Pennsylvania*, 522.
182. Historical Marker Database, "Marienville."
183. McKnight, *Pioneer Outline History of Northwestern Pennsylvania*, 327.
184. Switala, *Underground Railroad in Pennsylvania*, 39–40.

185. Wallace, *Indian Paths of Pennsylvania*, 27.
186. Ibid., 61.
187. Donehoo, *History of the Indian Villages and Place Names*, 66.
188. Ibid., 174.
189. McKnight, *Pioneer History of Jefferson County, Pennsylvania*, 284.
190. Wallace, *Indian Paths of Pennsylvania*, 174.
191. McKnight, *Pioneer Outline History of Northwestern Pennsylvania*, 319.
192. Ibid., 322.
193. Ibid., 323.
194. Scott, *History of Jefferson County, Pennsylvania*, 68.
195. Pure History, "Underground Railroad in Lycoming County, Penn."
196. Hunsinger, "Daniel Hughes."
197. Switala, *Underground Railroad in Pennsylvania*, 129–30.
198. Ibid., 130.
199. Ibid.
200. Pennsylvania Humanities Heartland Council, "Riots, Rumors and Stories."
201. *History of the Counties of McKean, Elk, and Forest*, 101.
202. Ibid.
203. Pettit, *Sketches in the History of the Underground Railroad*, 70–71.
204. Ibid.
205. Pennsylvania Wilds, "Potter County."
206. Switala, *Underground Railroad in Pennsylvania*, 27.
207. Pennsylvania State University, "Historical Sketches," 11.
208. *Potter Enterprise*, "John S. Mann House," 1.
209. Ibid., 11.
210. Ibid., 14, 15.
211. Tioga County, Pennsylvania website.
212. Donehoo, *History of the Indian Villages and Place Names*, 226.
213. Brown, *History of Tioga County, Pennsylvania*, 655.
214. Ibid., 655–56.
215. Ibid., 87.
216. Ibid.
217. Ibid., 88.
218. Ibid., 89.
219. Ibid., 90.
220. Switala, *Underground Railroad in Pennsylvania*, 130.
221. Free Dictionary, "Sugar Grove Underground Railroad Convention."
222. *Funk & Wagnalls New Encyclopedia*, "William Douglass," 132–33.
223. Free Dictionary, "Sugar Grove Underground Railroad Convention."
224. Ibid.
225. Pettit, *Sketches in the History of the Underground Railroad*, 15.
226. Ibid., 16.
227. Ibid., 17.
228. Ibid., 16.

Part IV

229. Fisher, "Going Home."

230. Lundy, *My Own Dearest Maggie*.

231. Ibid., 49, 50.

232. Ibid., 50.

233. Caldwell, *Caldwell's Atlas of Jefferson County, Pennsylvania*, 25.

234. *Brookville (PA) Republican*, "Captain Little Killed," 2.

235. Lundy, *My Own Dearest Maggie*, 62.

236. *Brookville (PA) Republican*, "Copperheads," 2.

237. Vinton and Allen, "Mr. Lonely."

238. Find A Grave, "George Washington Gathers."

239. Dickey, *History of the 103d Regiment, Pennsylvania*, 362.

240. Lambert, "When Johnny Comes Marching Home Again."

241. *Brookville (PA) Republican*, "All for McClellan," 1.

242. Ibid.

243. John Myers, "Myers Family Genealogy."

244. Bethlehem Evangelical Lutheran Church, "History of Bethlehem Evangelical Lutheran Congregation."

245. John Myers, "Myers Family Genealogy."

246. John Myers, "Myers Family Genealogy," Invalid Claim, Henry Myers, filed with Civil War Pensions, General Affidavit of Peter R. Reitz, January 28, 1877.

247. 1860 Federal Census.

248. *Brookville (PA) Republican*, "Fourth of July," 2.

249. *Wellsboro (PA) Gazette–Mansfield Advertiser*, "Grand Celebration of the 4th of July," 3.

250. John Myers, "Myers Family Genealogy," Invalid Claim.

251. 1880 Federal Census.

252. Joann Reitz, Reitz Family Tree.

253. *Jeffersonian Democrat*, "Peter R. Reitz, Deceased," 5.

254. 1870 Federal Census.

255. World Atlas, "Plummeting Fertility Rates in the United States."

256. Giesberg, "From Harvest Field to Battlefield," 160.

257. Ibid., 176.

258. Ibid., 159–60.

259. Ibid.

260. Ibid.

261. Ibid., 177.

262. Ibid., 160.

263. Ibid., 176.

264. *Brookville (PA) Republican*, "Aid Society," 2.

265. *Potter Journal and News*, "Ladies Aid Society," 2.

266. *Centre Democrat*, "Ladies Knitting Association," 2.

267. *Forest Republic*, "Side by Side in Long Sleep," 1.

268. Giesberg, "From Harvest Field to Battlefield," 161.

269. *Raftsman's Journal (Clearfield, PA)*, "In the Court, Campman vs. Campman," 2.

270. *Merriam-Webster*, "orphan," https://www.merrian-webster.com/describing/orphan.

271. Paul, *Pennsylvania's Soldiers' Orphan Schools*, preface, vii.

272. Ibid.

273. Pennsylvania Civil War, "Department of Soldiers' Orphans' Schools."

274. Paul, *Pennsylvania's Soldiers' Orphan Schools*, 44–45.

275. Ibid., 45.

276. Ibid., 49–50.

277. Ibid., 48.

278. Mansfield University Archived Catalogue, "History."

279. Paul, *Pennsylvania's Soldiers' Orphan Schools*, 480–83.

280. *Mansfield Advertiser*, "Mansfield Soldiers Orphan School," June 6, 1877, 3.

281. Ibid., June 12, 1878, 4.

282. Ibid., August 30, 1938, 7.

283. Ibid., April 14, 1886, 3.

284. *Wellsboro (PA) Gazette–Mansfield Advertiser*, "Edwin Goodwin and Nellie Mae Clark," 6.

285. *Wellsboro (PA) Gazette–Mansfield Advertiser*, "Mrs. Lucy Warren Rockwell," 7.

286. *Wellsboro (PA) Gazette–Mansfield Advertiser*, August 6, 1889, 3.

287. Hacker, "Census-Based Count of Civil War Dead."

288. Richardson, "Interview with J. David Hacker."

289. Ibid.

290. National Museum of Civil War Medicine, "Post-Traumatic Stress Disorder."

291. Horwitz, "Did Civil War Soldiers Have PTSD?"

292. National Museum of Civil War Medicine, "Post-Traumatic Stress Disorder."

293. Ibid.

294. Horwitz, "Did Civil War Soldiers Have PTSD?"

295. Ibid.

296. Ibid.

297. Ibid.

298. Ibid.

Part V

299. Wessman, *History of Elk County*, 99.

300. Ibid.

301. Ibid.

302. Ibid.

303. Ibid., 100.

304. Ibid.

305. Weidenboerner, "Historian Shocked FBI Searching."

306. Associated Press, "Hunters Sue for Records."

307. WTAJ, "Judge: FBI to Hand Over."
308. Miller, *John Wilkes Booth—Oilman*, 27.
309. *News-Herald (Franklin, PA)*, "Man No One Knows," 4.
310. Ibid.
311. Ibid.
312. Ibid.
313. *Potter Enterprise*, "From the County Bastille," 2.
314. *News-Herald (Franklin, PA)*, "Booth's Ghost Legend Revived," 2.
315. Parker, *Life of General Ely S. Parker*, 133.
316. Wallace, *Indians in Pennsylvania*, 8.
317. Ibid., 165–66.
318. Ibid., 170.
319. Seneca Nation of Indians, "Iroquois Confederacy, History."
320. City of Salamanca, New York, www.salmun.com.
321. Parker, *Life of General Ely S. Parker*, 3.
322. Ibid., 48.
323. Ibid., 96.
324. Ibid., 55.
325. Ibid., 101.
326. Ibid., 79.
327. Ibid., 99.
328. Ibid.
329. Ibid., 100.
330. Ibid.
331. Ibid., 102–3.
332. Ibid., 106.
333. Ibid., 115.
334. Ibid., 131.
335. Ibid., 142.
336. Ibid., 150.
337. U.S. Capitol Visitors Center, "Indian Citizenship Act."

Part VI

338. Wessman, *History of Elk County*, 164.
339. Ibid.
340. Ibid.
341. Ibid., 204.
342. Ibid., 163.
343. Ibid., 205.
344. Ibid., 167.
345. Hall and Schram, *Ridgway Cook Book*.
346. Ibid., 87.
347. Ibid., 8.

348. Ibid., 63.
349. Ibid., 43–44.
350. Ibid., 51.
351. Ibid., 150.
352. Ibid., 208.
353. Ibid., 292.

Conclusion

354. McPherson, *For Cause and Comrades*, 22.
355. Ibid., 118.
356. Library of Congress, "Grand Army of the Republic and Kindred Societies."
357. McPherson, "Out of War a New Nation."

BIBLIOGRAPHY

Aldrich, Lewis Cass. *History of Clearfield County, Pennsylvania.* Syracuse, NY: D. Mason, 1887.

Alexandria Archaeology Museum. "Union Hospitals in Alexandria." www. alexandriava.gov/historic/civilwar/UnionHospitals.

Allegheny College. "Elihu Chadwick, Jr., Introduction: April 20, 1861." In Civil War Letters, April 20, 2011. https://sites.allegheny.edu>civilwarletters>tag>elihu-chadwick-jr.

Associated Press. "Hunters Sue for Records on FBI's Civil War Gold Dig in Elk County." January 5, 2022.

Bates, Samuel P. *History of the Pennsylvania Volunteers, 1861–65.* Harrisburg, PA: B. Singerly, State Printer, 1869–71.

Beebe, Victor Llewellyn. *History of Potter County, Pennsylvania.* Coudersport, PA: Potter County Historical Society, 1934.

Bernard, Lou. "Celebrate Black History: Maria Molson 7 the Underground Railroad." Pennsylvania Wilds, February 28, 2022, https://pawilds.com/black-history-maria-molson-the-underground-railroad.

Bethlehem Evangelical Lutheran Church. "History of Bethlehem Evangelical Lutheran Congregation Near Ohl, Beaver Township, Jefferson County, PA, 1835–1935."

Brigham Young University Library. Thomas L. Kane, letter to Elizabeth Wood Kane, August 26, 1863. Thomas L. Kane Personal Papers, 1835–86. https://lib/byu.edu.

Britannica. "Era of Good Feelings." www.britannic.com/event/Era-of-Good-Feelings.

———. "Fort Sumter National Monument." www.britannica.com/event/Battle-of-Fort-Sumter.

———. "Fugitive Slave Acts." https://britannica.com/event/Fugitive-Slave-Acts.

Brookville (PA) Republican. "Aid Society." September 2, 1863.

———. "All for McClellan." October 19, 1864.

———. "Captain Little Killed." July 8, 1863.

———. "Copperheads." July 8, 1863.

———. "Fourth of July." June 21, 1865.

———. "New Publications: The Mystery Solved." April 6, 1864.

———. "Political Preachers." March 2, 1864.

———. "The War Commenced." April 18, 1861.

———. "What Is the Reason?" September 28, 1864.

Brown, R.C. *History of Tioga County, Pennsylvania*. Harrisburg, PA, 1897.

Caldwell, J.A. *Caldwell's Atlas of Jefferson County, Pennsylvania*. Condit, OH, 1878.

Cameron County Press. "Another Bucktail Gone." November 30, 1905.

Centre Democrat. "Ladies Knitting Association." September 26, 1861.

City of Salamanca, New York. www.salmun.com.

Clara Barton Missing Soldiers Office Museum. "Clara Barton Biography." www. clarabartonmuseum.org/bio.

Clarion (PA) Democrat. "Death of Benjamin Gardner." November 29, 1894.

Clearfield County. "The Best Place to Escape to in Pennsylvania." https:// visitclearfieldcounty.org/destinations/heritage/bloody-knox.

Clearfield (PA) Republican. "The War Begun." April 17, 1861.

Commonwealth of Pennsylvania. "State Symbols." www.pagov.guides/state-symbols.

Davis, A.J. *History of Clarion County, Pennsylvania*. Syracuse, NY: D. Mason & Company, 1887.

Dickey, Luther S. *History of the 103d Regiment, Pennsylvania Veteran Volunteer Infantry, 1861–1865*. Chicago, 1910.

Donehoo, George P. *A History of the Indian Villages and Place Names in Pennsylvania*. Lewisburg, PA: Wennawoods Publishing, 2010.

Elk County Advocate. "Notes." April 18, 1878.

———. "You Voted for the Draft." February 4, 1865.

Federal Census, 1850, Clarion, Clinton and Elk County, Pennsylvania.

Federal Census, 1860, Elk County and Jefferson County, Pennsylvania.

Federal Census, 1870, Elk County and Jefferson County, Pennsylvania.

Federal Census, 1880, Jefferson County, Pennsylvania.

Find A Grave. "George Washington Gathers (1817–1891)." www.findagrave.com.

———. "Rev Joseph Nesbitt." https://www.findagrave.com/memorial/102777781/ joseph-nesbitt.

Fisher, William Arms. "Going Home." Boston, July 21, 1922. Based on Antonin Dvorak's "Largo" theme from *Symphony No. 9*.

Forest Republic. "Side by Side in Long Sleep." March 27, 1912.

The Free Dictionary. "Sugar Grove Underground Railroad Convention." https:// encyclopedia2.thefreedictionary.com/Sugar+Grove+Underground+Railroad+ Convention.

Funk & Wagnalls New Encyclopedia. "Abolitionists." Vol. 1. New York, 1971, 1975.

———. "Civil War." Vol. 6. New York, 1971, 1975.

———. "Dred Scott Case." Vol. 8. New York, 1971, 1975.

———. "James Monroe." Vol. 16. New York, 1971, 1975.

———. "Knights of the Golden Circle." Vol. 14. New York, 1971, 1975.

———. "Louisiana Purchase." Vol. 15. New York, 1971, 1975.

———. "William Douglass." Vol. 8. New York, 1971, 1975.

Giesberg, Judith Ann. "From Harvest Field to Battlefield: Rural Pennsylvania Women and the U.S. Civil War." *Pennsylvania History: A Journal of Mid-Atlantic Studies* 72, no. 2 (2005). The Pennsylvania Historical Association, Villanova University.

Gosaloz, Emma. "Scholar Talks About Bellefonte's Underground Railroad Connections." *The Express*, May 3, 2016.

Grow, Matthew J. "Thomas L. Kane and Nineteenth-Century American Culture." *BYU Studies Quarterly* 48, no. 4, Article 3 (2009).

Hacker, J. David. "A Census-Based Count of Civil War Dead." History. www.history.com/news/civil-war-deadlier-than-previously-thought.

Hall, Mrs. J.K.P., and Mrs. J.M. Schram. *Ridgway Cook Book.* 2nd ed. New York: Francis F. Fitch Press, 1907.

Historical Marker Database. "Bucktail Monument." www.hmdb.org.

———. "Marienville." https://hmdb.org.

History of the Counties of McKean, Elk and Forest, Pennsylvania. Chicago: J.H. Beers & Company, Publishers, 1890.

History of the Counties of McKean, Elk, Cameron and Potter, Pennsylvania. Chicago: J.H. Beers & Company, Publishers, 1890.

History. "Congress Passes Civil War Conscription Act." www.history.com/this-day-in-history/congress-passes-civil-war-conscription-act-.

———. "This Day in History, the Underground Railroad." www.history.com/topics/black-history/underground.railroad.

Horwitz, Tony. "Did Civil War Soldiers Have PTSD?" *Smithsonian* (January 2015). https://www.smithsonianmag.com/history/ptsd-civil-wars-hidden-legacy-180953652.

Howard, Thomas O.R. *History of the Bucktails—Kane Rifle Regiment of Pennsylvania Reserve Corp, 13ᵗʰ Pennsylvania Reserves, 42 of the Line.* Philadelphia, PA: Philadelphia Electric Printing Company, 1873.

Hunsinger, Lou, Jr. "Daniel Hughes: Giant of Freedom Road." Handson Heritage. https://handsonheritage.com>daniel-hughes-giant-of-freedom-road.

Indiana State University Library. "Kate M. Scott's Sworn Statement." https://library.indstate.edu/about/units/rbsc/neff/kate_scott_statement.

Jeffersonian Democrat. "Death of Miss Kate Scott." April 20, 1911.

———. "Pennsylvania Memorial Home Receives Historical Marker." October 24, 2019.

———. "Peter R. Reitz, Deceased." May 10, 1900.

———. "The Summerless Year." April 10, 1878.

———. "A Watch Story." November 30, 1899.

Kane Area Development Center. "History of Kane." www.kanepa.com.

Kane Historic Preservation Society. "The Chapel." www.historickane.com/the-chapel.

Kane (PA) Republican. "Address of Robert Gray Taylor." January 9, 1934.

———. "Seen from the Hilltop." April 12, 1935.

Kinzua Bridge Foundation. "History." www.kinzuabridgefoundation.com/history.

Lambert, Louis (Patrick Gilmore), words and music. "When Johnny Comes Marching Home Again." Henry Tolman & Company, Boston, 1863.

Library of Congress. "Grand Army of the Republic and Kindred Societies: A Guide to Resources in the General Collections of the Library of Congress." https://guides.loc.gov/grand-army-0f-the-republic.

Llewellyn, Richard. *How Green Was My Valley.* New York: Macmillan Company, 1940.

Lundy, Jeffrey. *My Own Dearest Maggie: The Story of Civil War Captain Edwin Little and His Wife Maggie Told through His Letters Home.* Punxsutawney, PA, 2018. Jeffrey Lundy, lundyjeffrey@gmail.com.

Lycoming College. "About." www.lycoming.edu/about-lycoming/history.aspx.

Mansfield (PA) Advertiser. "Mansfield Soldiers' Orphan School." April 14, 1886.

———. "Mansfield Soldiers' Orphan School." June 6, 1877.

———. "Mansfield Soldiers' Orphan School." June 12, 1878.

Mansfield University Archived Catalogue. "History." www.mansfield.edu/mansfield-history.

McAllister, David. "Kane, Thomas Leiper." *Utah History Encyclopedia.* Salt Lake City: University of Utah Press, 1994. www.uen.org/utah-history-encyclopedia/k/Kane-Thomas.

McKnight, W.J. *A Pioneer History of Jefferson County, Pennsylvania and My First Recollections of Brookville, Pennsylvania, 1840–1843.* Philadelphia, PA: J.B. Lippencott, 1898.

———. *A Pioneer Outline History of Northwestern Pennsylvania.* Philadelphia, PA: J.B. Lippencott, 1905.

McPherson, James. *For Cause and Comrades: Why Men Fought in the Civil War.* New York: Oxford University Press, 1997.

———. "Out of War a New Nation." *Prologue Magazine* 42, no. 1 (Spring 2010). www.archives.gov/publications/prologue/2010/spring/newnation.

Meginness, John F. *History of Lycoming County, Pennsylvania.* Chicago: Brown, Runk & Company, 1892.

Miller, Ernest C. *John Wilkes Booth—Oilman.* New York: Exposition Press, 1947.

Mount Zion Historical Society. "Remembering Lieutenant Colonel Thomas B. Winslow (1836–1876)." https://mtzionhistoricalsociety.org.

Myers, John. "Myers Family Genealogy." In possession of author.

Myers, Kathy. "Winslow Genealogy." In possession of author.

National Archives and Records Administration. "Missouri Compromise (1820)." www.archives.gov/milestone-documents/missouri-compromise.

National Geographic. "Abolition and the Abolitionists." www.nationalgeographic.org/encyclopedia/abolition-and-abolitionist.

National Museum of Civil War Medicine. "Post-Traumatic Stress Disorder and the American Civil War." www.civilwarmed.org/ptsd.

National Wild and Scenic Rivers System. "Clarion River, Pennsylvania." https://www.rivers.gov/rivers/clarion.php.

News Herald (Franklin, PA). "Booth's Ghost Legend Revived." February 13, 1937.

———. "The Man No One Knows." February 15, 1971.

Parker, Arthur Caswell. *The Life of General Ely S. Parker, 1st Grand Sachem of the Iroquois and General Grant's Military Secretary*. Buffalo, NY: Buffalo Historical Society, 1919.

Parsons Holton, David. *Winslow Memorial*. New York, 1888.

Paul, James Laughery. *Pennsylvania's Soldiers' Orphan Schools*. Philadelphia: Claxton, Remsen & Haffelfinger, 1876.

Pennsylvania Civil War. "Department of Soldiers' Orphans' Schools." March 15, 1876. www.pacivilwar.com/orphans.

Pennsylvania Department of Transportation. "St. James Episcopal Church, Muncy, PA." National Register of Historic Places. www.gis.penndot/gov/crgisattachments/SiteResource.

Pennsylvania Great Outdoors Visitors Bureau. "Forest County." https://visitpago.com/counties/forest-county.

Pennsylvania Historic and Museum Commission. "Forty-Second Regiment (Bucktails), Pennsylvania Volunteers Records, Collection MG-234, Pennsylvania in the Civil War." www.phmc.pa.gov.

———. "Governor Andrew Gregg Curtin." www.phmc.state.pa.us/portal/communities/governors/1790-1876/andrew-curtin.html.

———. "A Guide for Classroom Teachers Researching the Civil War at the Pennsylvania State Archives." Introduction. www.phmc.pa.gov.

Pennsylvania Humanities Heartland Council. "Riots, Rumors and Stories: The Underground Railroad Period in Pennsylvania's Heartland: A Tour Guide." https://susquehannagreenway.org/sites/default/files/UGRRRoadtrip.pdf.

Pennsylvania State University. "The Founding of a Land Grant University—Penn State College of Agricultural Sciences." www.agsci.psu.edu/about/history/the-forming-of-a-land-grant-university.

———. "Historical Sketches of Potter County, Pennsylvania." https://digital.libraries.psu.edu/digital/collection.

Pennsylvania Wilds. "About." www.pawilds.com/about.

Pettit, Eber M. *Sketches in the History of the Underground Railroad*. Westfield, NY: Chautauqua Region Press, 1999.

Pike County Dispatch. "Died in Virginia." November 9, 1905.

Potter Enterprise (Coudersport, PA). "From the County Bastille." February 12, 1890.

———. "John S. Mann House." February 1, 1940.

Potter Journal and News (Coudersport, PA). "Ladies Aid Society." September 16, 1863.

The Progress. "North Star Way Picked as Name for Route 219." August 7, 1967.

Pure History. "Underground Railroad in Lycoming County, Penn." https://purehistory.org/underground-railroad-in-lycoming-county-penn.

Raftsman's Journal (Clearfield, PA). "Can It Be?" January 1, 1862.

———. "In the Court, Campman vs. Campman." August 9, 1866.

———. "Knights of the Golden Circle." April 18, 1860; July 25, 1860.

Reitz, Joann. Reitz Family Tree. Ancestry.com.

Richardson, Sara. "Interview with J. David Hacker: An Awful Tally Goes Higher." History.net. www.historynet.com/interview-j- david-hacker-awful-tally-goes-higher.

Schenck, J.S. *The History of Warren County, Pennsylvania*. Syracuse, NY: D. Mason & Company, 1887.

Scott, Kate M. *The History of Jefferson County, Pennsylvania*. Syracuse, NY: D. Mason & Company, 1888.

———. *History of the One Hundred and Fifth Regiment of Pennsylvania Volunteers*. Philadelphia, PA: New World Publishing Company, 1877.

Seneca Nation of Indians. "Iroquois Confederacy, History." https://sni.org/culture/history.

Susquehanna Greenway. "Riots, Rumors and Stories: The Underground Railroad and Abolitionists in the Valleys of the Susquehanna Region, Clinton County and the Underground Railroad." https://susquehannagreenway.org/sites.

Switala, William J. *Underground Railroad in Pennsylvania*. 2nd ed. Mechanicsburg, PA: Stackpole Books, 2008.

Taylor, Robert Gray. "Seen from the Hilltop." *Kane (PA) Republican*, January 9, 1934.

Tioga County, Pennsylvania. https://www.tiogacountypa.us.

Tioga Eagle (Wellsboro, PA). "Fugitive Slave Bill." October 16, 1850.

Turner, Edward Raymond. "The Negro in Pennsylvania, Slavery—Servitude—Freedom, 1639–1861." American Historical Association, Washington, 1911.

———. "Slavery in Pennsylvania." Diss., University of Michigan, 1911.

U.S. Capitol Visitors Center. "Indian Citizenship Act." www.visitthecapitol.gov/exhibitions/congress-and-world-ward-part-2/granting-citizenship-american-indians.

U.S. Census Bureau. "QuickFacts: Forest County, Pennsylvania." https://www.census.gov/quickfacts/forestcountypennsylvania.

Vinton, Bobby, and Gene Allen. "Mr. Lonely." *Roses Are Red (My Love)*, Epic Records, 1962.

Visit Central Pennsylvania. "Underground Railroad." www.visitcentral.pa.org/things-to-do/history-and-heritage/underground-railroad-tour.

Visit Clearfield County. "Bloody Knox." htpp://www.visitclearfieldcounty.org/parks_cabins_bloody_knox.

Visit Pennsylvania Great Outdoors. "Clarion County." www.visitpago.com/counties/clarion-county.

Wallace, Paul A.W. *Indian Paths of Pennsylvania*. Harrisburg, PA: Historical and Museum Commission, 2005.

———. *Indians in Pennsylvania*. Harrisburg, PA: Historical and Museum Commission, 1964.

Waters, Troy, Event Chairman for Downtown Bellefonte Inc. "Outdoor Adventures Expo." Pennsylvania Wilds, 2021. www.pawilds.com/outdoor-adventure-expo-2021.

Watson, Elmo Scott. "Last Survivors, Two Bucktails." *Braman (OK) Leader*, January 16, 1931.

Weidenboerner, Katie. "Historian Shocked FBI Searching Dents Run, Warns About Findings." *Courier-Express*, March 15, 2018.

Wellsboro (PA) Gazette–Mansfield Advertiser. "Edwin Goodwin and Nellie Mae Clark." August 24, 1927.

———. "Grand Celebration of the 4th of July." June 21, 1865.

———. "Mansfield Soldiers' Orphan School." August 30, 1938.

———. "Mrs. Lucy Warren Rockwell." September 12, 1934.

———. "Select Poetry, Where Are the Copperheads?" September 23, 1863.

———. "She Was a Civil War Nurse." September 15, 1920.

Wessman, Alice L., and Harriet Faust. *A Sesquicentennial History of Ridgway, Pennsylvania.* Ridgway, PA: Ridgway Publishing Company, 1974.

Wessman, Alice L., principal au., hist., ed. and comp. *A History of Elk County, Pennsylvania, 1981.* Ridgway, PA: Elk County Historical Society, 1981.

West, Julie, Communications Specialist, NPS Natural Sounds and Night Skies Division, Harriet Tubman National Historical Park. "North Star to Freedom." https://www.nps.gov/article/drinking.gourd.htm.

World Atlas. "Plummeting Fertility Rates in the United States: 1800 to 2020." www.worldatlas.com/articles/falling-fertility-rates-united-states.html.

World Population Review. "Population of Counties in Pennsylvania (2023)." https://worldpopulationreview.com/us-counties/states/pa.

WTAJ. "Judge: FBI to Hand Over Elk County Civil War Gold Hunt Records." April 19, 2022. www.wtaj.com.

ABOUT THE AUTHOR

Kathy Myers is a native of Ridgway, Elk County, Pennsylvania, where she has spent most of her life. She was the director of marketing at Elk County General Hospital in Ridgway, and prior to her retirement, she was the owner of Area Abstracting and Filing Service, a real estate settlement/title abstract company serving attorneys in Clearfield and Jefferson Counties.

A member of the seventh generation of her family to live in the Wilds, Myers is a historian, genealogist and writer who now resides in the Beechwoods of Jefferson County. She is a member of the General Society of Mayflower Descendants (GSMD), the founder and past governor of the Winslow Heritage Society, a member of the DuBois Area Historical Society and a member of the Jefferson County Historical Society. Myers is a juried member of the Wilds Cooperative of Pennsylvania.

She has published pieces in local newspapers; the *Mayflower Quarterly*, an international publication; and the *Watershed Journal*, a local literary publication. In 2021, she authored *Historic Tales of the Pennsylvania Wilds*, published by Arcadia Publishing/The History Press.

Myers served her community as president of the Ridgway Area School Board, president of the Elk County General Hospital Auxiliary and president of the Elk County Recreation and Tourist Council. She served on the GSMD 2014 Congress Planning Committee, was a chairperson of the GSMD Marketing Committee and served as membership chair for the Society of Mayflower Descendants in Pennsylvania, where she also acted as assistant to the historian. She was regent of the DuBois-Susquehanna Chapter of the Daughters of the American Revolution.

She is married to her high school sweetheart, John; they are the parents of one son and have two grandsons.